PSYCH YOURSELF IN

HYPNOSIS AND HEALTH

MARLENE E. HUNTER
B.A.,M.D.,C.F.P.C.(c)

EDITOR: BETTY KELLER
ILLUSTRATIONS: JILL TEBBITT

PSYCH YOURSELF IN
HYPNOSIS AND HEALTH

ISBN 0-9691820-0-7

Publisher:

    SeaWalk Press Ltd.
    2539 Nelson Ave.
    West Vancouver, B.C. V7V 2R5

Typesetting: Glassford Press Ltd.

Printing: First Folio Printing Co. Ltd.

Printed and Bound in Canada

FOR
REDNER

Acknowledgements:
- A special acknowledgement to Dr. F.W. Hanley
  for all his teaching over the years.
- To the members of the SunCoast Writers Forge
  for their time and energy.
- To Jill Tibbitt
  for her provocative art work.
- To Betty Keller
  for sitting me down and making me do it, thus bringing about the
  transformation of a decade of "Some day ...." 's into a real book.

INTRODUCTION

The pudgy lady in the black coat was very determined to set me straight.

"I told you, Doctor Hunter, and I'll tell you again," she said, thumping her purse on my desk to emphasize her words, "I haven't slept a minute in the last seven months! Don't waste my time with this gobbledegook hypnosis nonsense of yours! What I need is sleeping pills!"

She wasn't the first patient to tell me I was wasting her time, and I guess she won't be the last, so what does make me persist with this gobblegook hypnosis of mine?

First, because every time I give a prescription for pills to someone like the lady in the black coat, I am only colluding to mask their real problems.

Second, I persist because I believe that good medical practice demands that I help my patients to find out what has caused the situation that they find themselves in and then that I help them to work out a better way of coping with it.

Third, I persist because I have always believed that old saw that says if you give a man a fish, you may stave off his hunger for three days, but if you teach him how to fish he can provide his own fish for the rest of his life. If I can teach my patients how to keep healthy and resolve some of their problems through hypnosis, I have given them the most important tool they need to take responsibility for their own good health for the rest of their lives.

★ ★ ★

I began using hypnosis in my medical practice shortly after I returned to Canada from Kenya in 1971. At that time, I did a lot of work in the emergency room of Lions Gate Hospital, and every day I dealt with children who were scared stiff of the strange smells and the strange people wearing strange clothes in strange surroundings. As if it wasn't bad enough that these children were coming in sick or injured, they were faced with this unnecessary distress as well.

I remember one particular youngster who had fallen off his bike on his way home from Kindergarten. He had a huge gash in his knee. His mother had seen him fall and had carried him home to clean the grit out of the cut. Her efforts had only made it more painful, so in a flap herself by this time, she had bundled him up and brought him into emergency.

Unfortunately, the nurse on the desk that day was unusually officious and starchy as she came to take him from his mother, so by the time he arrived in the operaring room where I was checking out the suture tray, he was sobbing incoherently with fright. Nothing I could say or do would calm him. The nurse "bundled" him down into the restraining sheet as I talked soothingly into his ear, but he just kept on screeching. And all the time I worked putting in the local, cleansing the wound and suturing it, he continued to howl.

There's got to be a better way to help these kids with their fears, I decided. *I cannot continue contributing to this sort of brutality*.

Shortly after that, by some kind of serendipity, a brochure arrived on my desk announcing that the American Society of Clinical Hypnosis would be holding a workshop in Vancouver in the near future. My subconscious said, *"This is it!"* And it was. Not only was it the solution to some of my problems in the emergency room, but it soon became increasingly evident that I could use it effectively in my office practice. As the years went by, I found that the more I introduced people to hypnosis in my practice, the more I was asked for further reading material on the subject.

And I found that although there are a few good books on self-hypnosis available, none of them have really stressed the point of view which seems of the utmost importance to me: namely, that *most human beings are totally unaware of the many, many inner resources that are at their disposal, and they do not realize that they can get in touch with these resources and use them to improve and maintain good health*.

I have not found a book on self-hypnosis which explains that *how we behave and how we speak reflects our subconscious thoughts and feelings* and that *when we gain insight into these thoughts and feelings, we can understand ourselves and our responses better.* This improved understanding will enable us to recognize the need for change in our lives and to perceive how that can come about. A great many of these subconscious thoughts are reflected in our physical and emotional health; for instance, when we say that something "makes us sick", we often go on to prove that it literally does just that. But once we understand this correlation, we can start changing the process for ourselves.

We allow ourselves to fall into patterns of thought and behaviour, but the only time we pay any attention to these patterns is when we become conscious that it is time to "get out of our rut". So far I have not found a book on hypnosis which explains that we can make good use of the patterns we are in, that we can consider them and re-evaluate them from a different perspective, the perspective of the present, and that we can utilize that re-evaluation to modify and enrich our lives. I call this process *spiralling*. It is the concept of the individual *coming around again to the same place in his pattern of experience but on a different level* so that he is able to re-assess that pattern from a new angle.

So how do these concepts fit into hypnosis?

Man's conscious mind hampers his comprehension of these processes and patterns. It confines him to understanding only from a logical or intellectual approach. Therefore, he must open up a place for intuitive knowledge and response, and the best way to do this is through hypnosis. He can utilize it to gain insight and to understand the "getting-in-touch-with-the-resources" process.

All hypnosis is really self-hypnosis. While it is useful to have a thoroughly trained professional to get you started or to offer suggestions and/or advice on a particularly difficult problem, your hypnosis is always self-induced. Some people find it is helpful to have a cassette tape to encourage relaxation or to offer suggestions or guidelines; I have made a number of these tapes and they are now available commercially. But whether you work with a professional hypnotherapist or make use of tapes to relax, you will find that *self-hypnosis will be the tool you need* for a more responsible, healthier future.

TABLE OF CONTENTS

1. *Screening out the "zonkers"* — Responding to hypnotic suggestion
2. *Getting things into focus* — Focussing on the inner self to bring on a hypnotic state.
3. *Measuring the altered states* — Measuring brain wave activity during hypnosis
4. *Demonstrating Control* — Gaining control over bodily functions
5. *What's going to happen to me in there?* — Establishing a relationship of trust with your hypnotherapist
6. *Whatever Turns you on* — Enjoying self-hypnosis

1. *Imaginary Versus Psychosomatic Illness* — Understanding the interaction of the psyche and the soma
2. *The Theory of Psychosomatic Disease* — Understanding the function of the neurotransmitters
3. *Psychosomatic Disease and You* — Understanding stress

Chapter Ten: More Habits and Hypnosis — 121

Chapter Eleven: The Future — 131

Index

Chapter One

I'm In Control Here

It was the evening "happy hour" at a conference for family physicians where I had gone to give a workshop on hypnotherapy. As usual, none of us could let the day's topics die, and I was entertaining a group with the story of my first *warts patient.*

"His mother came to see me because she had heard that hypnosis worked on warts. I had never dealt with warts up till that time, but I knew of people who had, so I agreed to see him. The child was about ten or eleven and he had a terrible crop of warts all over both hands, but like all children, he was very interested in hypnosis. After only two sessions I felt that we had done all that was necessary. I invited him to come back when the warts were all gone to show me his nice looking hands.

'When is that going to be?' I asked, and he gave me a date about three weeks away. 'Right,' I said. 'Let's go and make an appointment with my receptionist right now.'

I noticed that Marsha looked a little skeptical but I let it go. Three weeks later, the boy came back to show me his hands with their lovely clear skin.

'Congratulations!' I said. 'Isn't that wonderful! I knew you could do it!'

He marched out of my office a very happy boy, but as I emerged behind him I saw that Marsha was looking at me with her eyebrows raised.

'They're all gone?' she asked.

'All gone!'

She shook her head and shuddered. 'That's CR-R-R-EEPY!' she said."

My audience laughed and after a minute I continued, "She could understand hypnosis working for pain control or getting rid of headaches or helping people to sleep better, but she couldn't accept actual physical change. And it didn't even help when I explained that getting rid of warts was just the same as getting rid of headaches, because warts, after all, are only the physical signs of an allergic reaction to a virus."

At the end of my story, one of my listeners interrupted with a question.

"And what about phobias?" he asked. "Can you make any headway with things like claustrophobia?"

Realizing that he hadn't attended my workshop that morning, I went over what I had discussed, but before I had finished, he interrupted again.

"What about somebody who is afraid of flying?"

"Sure," I said. "I get a lot of patients with that problem."

He turned his attention away from me then and beamed from ear to ear at a beautiful woman who stood across from him. "You see, she *can* help you!" he announced.

I could feel her withdrawing. "Oh no," she said. "Oh no, I would never do that!"

This beautiful woman was the doctor's wife and it turned out that she had such a fear of flying that she could never go anywhere with him. Apparently the last time she had tried to accompany him to a conference, she had spent three hours before the flight crying uncontrollably and in the end had abandoned the plan to go with him. She was only at this conference because it was in her own home town.

Her fear came from the fact that she could not bear the thought of losing control of the situation. She could not fly in a plane because she could not pilot it. She would drive a car herself but would not ride in a car as a passenger. For the same reason, she would not even consider submitting to hypnosis.

"Nobody's taking control of me that way," she said.

"Where did you get the idea that you'd lose control in hypnosis?" I asked.

The lady explained that she had seen a stage hypnotist performing some years earlier and had been terrified by what she saw. She described how he had told the members of the audience to clasp their hands together and how they had been unable to unclasp them. He told them to hold their hands up in the air, about two feet apart with the palms facing, then suggested that they would find their hands irresistibly drawn together. And they *were*! After a while he invited some audience members to the stage and there he "hypnotized" one lady so that she made her body as stiff as a board. Two men had placed her so that her head rested on one chair and her feet on another, and *then* he stood on her stomach!

But the worst part of the evening came when he told a group of people under hypnosis that they would need to use the toilet when they came out of hypnosis but that they would not be able to leave the stage. And so the whole group sat squirming on stage while the audience laughed at them. Finally he sent them to their seats with post-hypnotic suggestions that made them leap to their feet and say and do silly things whenever he gave the signal.

The doctor's wife was quite sure that she knew everything there was to know about hypnosis after this experience, and she was determined never to allow herself to be controlled in that way.

"What you saw was the worst kind of stage hypnotist," I told her. "Not all hypnotists are that unscrupulous."

"What do you mean — "unscrupulous?" she asked.

"Well, stage hypnotists only use the hypnotic phenomena that they can build an entertainment around. The good ones do it in a way that is not really offensive, but the bad ones are thoroughly objectionable. They humiliate and degrade the "volunteers" they get from the audience."

1. Screening Out The "Zonkers"

Stage hypnotists depend on the fact that a very small part of the population is able to go into deep levels of hypnosis without previous training or experience. I call these people "zonkers".

A good hypnotist can screen these people from his audience by suggesting various simple dissociation "tricks" and watching carefully to see who will respond consistently to his suggestions. He may say: "Your rights hands are getting lighter and lighter. Soon those hands will rise *by themselves* into the air!" Then he simply makes a mental note of the hands that are raised. In an audience of three thousand people, there are bound to be twenty or thirty "zonkers" who will respond to all his suggestions, and this is more than enough to stage the most extravagant show.

However, even a "zonker" always has a choice of whether or not he will go into hypnosis, and *how* he is going to respond while in hypnosis, and *whether or not* he will remain in hypnosis. Even when he appears not to, he always has a choice, because it is *absolutely impossible* for one person to hypnotize another. The most that a "hypnotist" can do is help his subject into a hypnotic state, and he can only do that if the subject is willing to let it happen.

All hypnosis, therefore, is really *self-hypnosis*. Even the people that the doctor's wife had watched on stage had not lost control, but instead had given implicit consent to follow the hypnotist's suggestions. Subconsciously, most of them were absolutely thrilled by the opportunity to perform, a thing that they would never do in "real life". They needed an excuse to get up there. Others allowed themselves to take part, just for the fun of it. And it *can* be fun!

"But those people who needed to use the toilet!" said the doctor's wife. "Surely they didn't consent to that! It was humiliating!"

"Probably more humiliating for you than for them," I told her. "They weren't consciously humiliated at all because they were simply accepting a post-hypnotic suggestion. Of course, at *some* level of consciousness they knew exactly what was happening because in hypnosis we are *never un*conscious. Hypnosis is an *altered* state of consciousness or awareness."

"What do you mean by *altered state*?" she asked.

"I mean that the subject always knows who he is and where he is and what he is doing, even though he may not appear to. He is *not* in a coma, but his usual interest in what is going on around him has diminished. He is now more interested in what's going on within himself."

"But do you remember what has happened to you in hypnosis?"

"Yes. But many people when they first come out of hypnosis, don't remember everything that's happened. Of course, it all comes back after a while if you want it to. "Zonkers" sometimes deliberately choose not to remember what has happened during hypnosis.''

2. Getting Things Into Focus

"Hypnosis," I continued when I saw that the lady was still un-convinced, "is *not magic*. It is simply a means by which the in-dividual can focus his attention in an ever-narrowing direction so that everything outside of that focus becomes more and more remote. It's not an unusual phenomenon. All of us have ex-perienced it; we've just known it by other names."

The man who drives six blocks past his house because his mind was on something else. The boy who daydreams on his way from school and gets home an hour and a half late. The woman who doesn't hear her name called when she's reading a novel, because she is "in another world". The man who focusses on a memory of the past and blots out the present. The child involved in a television program who forgets to come to the dinner table. These are all *spontaneous hypnotic phenomena*. We call them day-dreaming, or being lost in thought, or being in another world, or being in a brown study, but we simply mean that these people are concentrating their thoughts on something remote from that which is going on around them, concentrating on something within themselves.

In hypnosis we deliberately enter this altered stage of con-sciousness, but it's not the only way we can enter. Deep prayer can bring on the same effect because the person praying shuts out the world around him. The contemplative relaxation of yoga or of meditation are both altered stages of consciousness as well.

When a patient comes to me for hypnotherapy, I help him into a hypnotic state by focussing his attention in some way. I may simply talk to him in a lulling monotone so that the drone of my voice will help him to go off into a daydreamy state. It's just like a mother soothing a child. Or like the monotonous voices of a few lecturers I could name!

Or I may use an eye-fixation technique, focussing the patient's vision on a light or on a point on the wall. Usually, however, I use my thumb — something that I always have with me — bringing it slowly closer until it rests on the patient's forehead. Many therapists use a rhythmic moving object like a swinging pendulum or a strobe light; both of these have the same effect as the steady swish-swish of the windshield wipers on a rainy night. Anything that appears *again* and *again* and *again* holds potential for hypnotic induction.

Some techniques bring on a hypnotic state faster than others. A lulling voice telling you to relax and imagine yourself floating on a cloud will usually take longer to induce a hypnotic state than a strobe light will because the subject will try to get away from the strobe light and "go into himself" as quickly as possible. That is why stage hypnotists prefer to use swinging pendulums and rapid eye-fixation techniques; they haven't time to relax their subjects. They need fast results to keep their audiences' interest.

In self-hypnosis, the individual simply makes use of any inner focussing technique that suits him. It's really a very personal thing, depending largely on how he forms images in his mind. Many people form visual images, conjuring up pictures in their minds. Others form "kinesthetic" images, that is, images of what they are feeling within their bodies. A third group forms auditory or sound images. Occasionally, some of the other senses such as touching or tasting evoke images, but most people have one of these three main ways of forming images — pictures, feelings, or sound — and the others are used only to enrich the basic picture.

So if you ask a group of people to think of themselves riding a bicycle, those that think in pictures would either see themselves riding the bike or would see the scenery which they were riding past. The "kinesthetic" ones would feel the wind in their faces, their bodies moving on the bicycle, the movement of their legs going up and down. The "sound" people would hear the sound of the tires whirring along the road, the lapping of the water on the shore, the cry of the gulls.

Although going into hypnosis is a very personal experience, the therapist can get a good idea of how his patients form images by the expressions that they use. The visual imagers tend to express themselves in phrases like "I see what you mean". Kinesthetic imagers might say "I don't feel that's the right thing for me", while if the patient says "I hear what you are suggesting to me", he is probably an auditory imager.

Whether the thing that you focus on in hypnosis is something your hypnotherapist suggested to you or something you thought of yourself, it has to be something that is comfortable to you, something that you are willing to accept. Your mind will refuse to focus on something that is uncomfortable to you. For instance, a person who has had a near drowning will not want to focus on the thought of floating down a river or going into a whirlpool!

3. Measuring The Altered States

"How could you tell if I was in hypnosis?" asked the doctor's wife.

"I would watch for changes in your breathing and facial expression. But aside from that, hypnosis does cause a least one measurable physiological change in the body: the pattern of the brain waves alters."

Normal thought is known as cortical activity and it produces "beta" waves in the brain. These show up on an electroencephalogram as rapid frequency spikes. "Alpha" waves are considerably slower and indicate a calming of the brain's activity. People who are in alpha rhythm may be in meditation, yoga, deep prayer, or a light or relaxation level of hypnosis. "Theta" waves are even slower than alpha waves; people who are in theta wave activity may be almost ready to fall asleep, may be in a coma, or in deep levels of hypnosis. "Delta" waves are the slowest of all and indicate that the person has gone to sleep.

"Zonkers" quickly achieve slower rhythms without necessarily having had previous experience in hypnosis, but many people who begin by being so-called "light subjects", can go deeper as they become more experienced or more comfortable with hypnosis.

My own normal level of hypnosis takes me into the theta range. On one occasion when my colleagues and I were doing research in the area of brainwave activity, I volunteered to submit to an e.e.g. I remember two things about this experiment very vividly. I remember the chap who was operating the e.e.g. commenting, "Well, she's either in coma or she's dead!" I felt that this was very unkind of him!

What had upset the e.e.g. operator was the fact that under hypnosis I lose my beta waves very quickly and enter the alpha rhythm state, and then as my hypnosis deepens, I show more and more theta waves.

After I had entered the alpha range, one of my colleagues with my permission began directing the experiment, and guided me into a deeper level of hypnosis. The e.e.g. changed to theta waves. It had been decided that I would be asked to solve mathematical problems; my answers would be checked on a pocket calculator. My colleague instructed me that I would see the answers written on a blackboard, and this is exactly what happened. I am no mathematical whiz but I was reading the answers off my mental blackboard faster than my colleague could get the answers on his calculator!

When I thought about it later, I realized that the hand I had been watching had written the answers starting from the right hand side of the board and working to the left, just as if the owner of the hand had been working out complicated multiplication problems. I just waited until the hand had finished writing the last number and then read off the answer.

I realized as well that I had recognized the hand that was producing the answers. It belonged to my much loved Grade Five teacher. I recognized her freckles.

When I came out of hypnosis, I had a look at the e.e.g. tracing and I could see immediately where I had gone into hypnosis because the pattern change was so marked. Then further on, it was equally marked where my colleague had taken over because the pattern showed mostly theta waves with only a few alpha waves. But the most interesting aspect of the whole experiment for me was the fact that I had been performing cortical activity when I had not been operating in the range of normal cortical activity brainwaves. This would seem to suggest that I could not have been thinking! However, what it really points up is the fact that since hypnosis is an altered state of consciousness, instead of the usual *conscious* thinking process, the person under hypnosis can do work which is apparently cortical with a different or altered brain wave activity.

Experiments have also shown that subjects who learn meditation are able to increase the number and extent of the alpha and theta wave changes as they become more experienced. The more they meditate, the more commonly the alpha and theta rhythm changes occur.*

"But you are probably not a zonker like me," I reassured the doctor's wife. "At least you chose not to respond to the hypnotist's suggestions, didn't you?"

"Well, I wasn't going to make a fool of myself!" she said. And then she smiled. "Oh, I see what you mean. That proves your point about choice, doesn't it?"

"Yes."

"You know, I wouldn't mind *watching* while you put someone under hypnosis," she said hesitantly. "Just to see how it was different to what I saw on stage..."

---

* West, Michael A., "Meditation and the E.E.G.", *Psychological Medicine*, 1980, Volume X, pages 369-375.

"I think that could be arranged," I said. "Then afterwards, if you like, you could talk with the person and find out how he felt about the experience."

"Would he remember?" she asked.

"If he wants to. But remember some people may choose to forget for a while. They want to hold onto the nice feeling for a bit before they deal with the details."

"How would you know what I was thinking when I was under hypnosis?"

"I would ask you questions."

"How would I answer?"

Generally speaking, I explained, people in light levels of hypnosis find talking quite easy, but the deeper they go the less inclined they are to talk because talking takes too much energy. So very often when a subject is in a deep level of hypnosis or if I feel that talking might interrupt his concentration, I suggest that he answer my questions by "ideomotor responses" — movements triggered by his ideas. Before he goes into hypnosis and again during hypnosis, I explain that the ideas that he wishes to communicate will cause his fingers to move. I ask him to tell me which finger is going to be his Yes-finger. "Just let the finger move itself, because this will be your subconscious mind making the decision."

Then the subject and I wait until the subconscious causes a small fluttery movement in one finger. Then I ask which the No-finger will be, again waiting for a fluttery response. Finally I ask which finger will be the I-don't-want-to-answer-that-right-now-finger because this is a legitimate answer during therapy. Sometimes the subject will use this answer when I have asked a question which he felt was none of my business, but usually it is used when the subject knows the answer but does not want to think about it yet. This gives him the opportunity to temporize a little longer, and tells me as the therapist that I should not ask anything more about that topic, at least for a while.

Sometimes people answer with ideomotor responses without pre-arrangement. The head will nod just a little or the pattern of the breathing will change in response to certain questions, and the therapist understands that the subconscious has been stirred in some way. Occasionally, people will speak in hypnosis while their fingers are giving a different answer. I might ask, "Are you ready to deal with this problem now?" and the subject will answer "Yes" at the same time as his No-finger is waggling for all it's worth. Then I know that the topic will have to wait because the subconscious is not yet prepared to deal with the problem.

4. Demonstrating Control

By the time the "happy hour" was over, it had been agreed that the doctor's wife would attend a hypnosis session that I was presenting the following morning. Just by coincidence, I was intending to demonstrate how people can gain greater control over their bodies, especially those physical things that they normally think of as uncontrollable or beyond conscious control. In this kind of demonstration, the object is to illustrate that pain can be controlled, so I arrange for someone in the audience to poke me with a sterile needle after I have gone into hypnosis. This also gives me a chance to demonstrate the control of bleeding because under hypnosis I can turn the bleeding on or off, depending on what I am asked to do by those around me. In fact, if I am poked in two different places, I can have one puncture bleed and the other not bleed. People with exceptional control, who have been punctured by a needle which goes in one spot and out another, can have one or the other, or both holes, or neither hole bleed.

One of my colleagues has this kind of control over his blood vessels, and one one occasion when a group of us were demonstrating to a professional meeting, a skeptic in the audience volunteered to be the one to wield the needle. In his enthusiasm to prove that the bleeding could *not* be stopped, he stuck it right through a vein and left the needle in it so that the blood went drip, drip, drip off the end of it like a leaky faucet. The colleague who was conducting the demonstration leaned over the subject and said quietly, "Okay now, Bob, stop the bleeding, stop the bleeding." And he did. Then the needle was taken out. Bob was still in hypnosis.

At this point, as I was sitting right next to him, I heard him saying very faintly, "Please tell me to stop the hematoma!" I looked down at the hand that had been punctured and saw that there was a great big bump coming up where the blood had collected under the skin. I said, "Stop the hematoma, Bob, make it go down." And he did. At the end of the day, he didn't even have a bruise.

There are practical applications for this ability to stop bleeding. When I was completing my daughter Rachel's quilt, and sewing

the final strips on with the sewing machine, the machine needle went through my thumbnail. Now, Rachel's quilt is pale blue combined with very soft pastel patchwork patterns and I was darned if I wanted blood on it after all my work! As soon as I realized what I had done, I ordered myself to stop bleeding, and when that was established I told myself to be comfortable. As a result, it didn't bleed and it didn't hurt, and the quilt was saved.

This ability to stop bleeding is not difficult to master and many of my patients have put it to good use. One lady who did very well with it had come to me for hypnotherapy prior to surgery. She recognized the need for the operation but she was frightened nevertheless, and wanted to learn to control her anxiety. We had two or three sessions before surgery so that she went into the hospital with only mild apprehension which she coped with very well.

During surgery we ran into a lot of adhesions and because we had to separate the adhesions there was a tremendous amount of bleeding. She just *bled* and *bled* and *bled* and really obscured the operating field. Finally, I leaned over and said to her, "Mary, stop bleeding. The blood is getting in the way and we can't see what we're doing." And within the next thirty or forty seconds, the bleeding began to subside. We continued the operation with no further problems.

Later that afternoon, Mary's husband phoned me to say, "I've just been up to see Mary and the first thing she said when she came out of the anaesthetic was 'What went wrong in the operation?' I told her that nothing went wrong and she was just fine, but she said, 'Yes, I'm fine *now*, but what went wrong when they were operating?"

After office hours I went up to see her myself and she asked again, "What went wrong in surgery?" I explained about the bleeding and she said, "Oh, I knew there was something!" She was pleased that through her hypnosis, she had actually become one of the operating team.

When I saw her again some weeks later, I read the note to her that I had received from her surgeon describing how extremely smoothly her post-operative course had gone — much more smoothly than he had anticipated — and how very quickly she had resumed her normal activities.

She just chuckled and said, "He just doesn't understand that you and I had an agreement!"

5. What's Going To Happen To Me In There?

For the doctor's wife who *did* go on to conquer her fear of flying and for Mary who assisted in her own operation, finding hypnosis was a happy ending, but many people never break through their barrier of fear. They are afraid of being manipulated in hypnosis, of being controlled. They ask, "What's going to happen to me in there once the door closes on the treatment room? What will this hypnotherapist do to me when she gets me in her power?"

The first thing such people can do to allay their fears is check the credentials of the person to whom they go for hypnotherapy. Since this is medical science's way of harnessing hypnosis, your hypnotherapist should not only be trained thoroughly in hypnosis, but also have a strong background in psychology so that he understands how the body responds to and works with the mind or the spirit. Anyone operating in this field without a solid understanding of psychology is like a mechanic who doesn't really understand *why* the internal combustion engine works.

In the second place, you can check on the professional societies that your hypnotherapist belongs to. If he is a member of the American Society of Clinical Hypnosis, or the Society of Clinical and Experimental Hypnosis in the United States, or the Canadian Society of Clinical Hypnosis or one of its provincial branches in Canada, you can be sure that he is a trained hypnotherapist because these are all highly ethical professional societies which demand professional accreditation of their membership. They accept only medical doctors, psychologists, and psychiatrists who can show proof of their training in hypnosis. A special branch of each society is reserved for dentists who use hypnosis in their dental practices; these people are not trained in psychology and therefore limit their area of expertise to dentistry.

Finally, in any relationship of this kind, you should trust your emotional reactions. If you are to receive maximum benefit from your hypnotherapy sessions, it is very important that you have trust and confidence in your therapist. Otherwise, you will probably not go into very deep levels of hypnosis, not because you will be unable to, but because you choose not to. Perhaps you will be afraid of losing control of the situation or of divulging secrets that you do not trust your therapist to hear.

On the other hand, of course, the hypnotherapist must have regard for his patient. One of my very few "failures" in hypnotherapy was a gentleman who came to me for help with headaches. He disliked taking medication and felt that hypnosis would help him avoid it. He was a perfectly co-operative subject, but at the first session he did not go into hypnosis very deeply. I was not worried because this is quite common, but when we made no progress at the second session either, I realized that something was definitely wrong.

After he left, I went into hypnosis myself and began asking myself what was going wrong, but before I had finished phrasing the question, I knew the answer. *I didn't like my patient.* I felt he was superficial and condescending. I didn't quite trust him, in fact. So the next time we met, I suggested that he go to another therapist. He did, and got good relief from his headaches.

In going to a hypnotherapist and agreeing to use hypnosis to deal with your problem, you make a conscious contract with your hypnotherapist. You are agreeing to consider some suggestions under hypnosis. The *subconscious contract* is usually arrived at later. When I am inducing hypnosis during therapy, I suggest to my patients that when they close their eyes it will be a signal that they are ready to go into some level of hypnosis, whatever level is appropriate for them at that time. If a bond of trust has been established, that second contract, the subconscious one, will be entered into implicitly at that time. If trust has not been established, there will be little progress in therapy.

As for what is going to happen once the door has closed on the treatment room, that depends largely on the culture in which the hypnosis is practiced. In some middle European countries, the patient who arrives in his therapist's office with a headache might be

ordered under hypnosis: "YOU WILL STOP HAVING THIS HEADACHE! THE HEADACHE WILL GO!" This is a very authoritarian approach but it is suitable for the culture in which it is used. In some parts of Africa the hypnotherapist would liken the headache to demons that have to be released from their prison, so he might take himself and his patient into a hypnotic state where they could imagine the demons being released. It's very flamboyant but culturally correct.

In North America, hypnotherapy is generally very permissive. Suggestions are given in a very open-ended way in order to allow the individual to make his own amendments, modifications, and adjustments. For instance, I might say to a patient, "Here are some things you might want to think about just to get your mind working in that direction," or "I have a suggestion to make that you may find useful." In this way, the patient knows that he is being given the opportunity to *choose* whether or not he will use that suggestion or some part of it.

The therapist is very careful to phrase all his questions and suggestions in a positive mode.

Rather than saying, "You will not need a sleeping pill to-night," he must say, "You can sleep well to-night."

Instead of "Do not be anxious," he must turn the idea around to "Enjoy being more self-confident!"

"You will not feel pain" becomes "You can feel more comfortable".

The reason for this subterfuge is that in hypnosis it is the *subconscious mind* which responds, and since the subconscious only deals with images, metaphors, and analogies, it does not hear negatives. In this respect, it is like an analog computer. Only the thinking part of the mind, the conscious part which deals in language and logic, understands negatives, rather like a digital computer. So while the conscious mind understands "Don't worry!" the subconscious only hears "---- worry!" and proceeds to respond as ordered.

Many people never go beyond a light level of hypnosis, but this is no bar to good results in hypnotherapy because the depth of the trance or state of hypnosis and the effectiveness of the therapy do not seem to be related. "Zonkers", therefore, do not necessarily get better therapeutic results than the people who stay in the lighter levels of hypnosis. The subject goes to whatever level of hypnosis that he finds comfortable and he changes that level whenever he chooses. Even if he gets "out of his depth" inadvertently, he will always quickly return to a level where he can work most comfortably and effectively.

Occasionally, a person who has come to me for hypnotherapy resists hypnosis when we actually begin or stays at a very light level. One or two have even resisted in more overt ways such as beginning to talk just when I have begun therapeutic suggestions, or getting an attack of the fidgets. Obviously the bond of trust has not been established, and the patient is unable to conquer the hidden fear that I might be taking over.

These people come out of hypnosis quickly, and as they leave my office, they may remark something like, "Isn't it too bad it didn't work, doctor?" This is their way of keeping their pride intact. They've tried hypnosis and it didn't work!

In fact, I can only think of two or three cases in all my years of using hypnotherapy where it truly "failed to work". In each case, the subject began to go into hypnosis and brought himself out of it almost immediately because the experience reminded him of something frightening from the past which he may or may not have been consciously aware of: a near drowning, anaesthetic in childhood surgery, or night terrors as a child. These events were experienced as hypnotic phenomena at the time, so that when the person started to go into hypnosis as an adult, the subconscious remembered the earlier event and said, "Oh, no, not this again!" And promptly withdrew from hypnosis. As this chain of events happens in a matter of seconds, the person is under the impression that he never went into hypnosis at all.

Very often people come out of their first hypnotherapy session firmly convinced that they have not experienced hypnosis. Usually they say something like "Well, I certainly felt very comfortable and relaxed but I wasn't in hypnosis, you know, because I was quite aware of everything that was going on!" My reply is "Yes, it is a nice comfortable feeling, isn't it? How long do you think you were lying there?" And they are surprised to learn that it was a half an hour instead of the five or ten minutes that they supposed.

Time in hypnosis is often very distorted because it has no relevance. Consequently, you lose all track of time, just as you do when you concentrate intently during conscious activity. We acknowledge this phenomenon with the cliche about time passing quickly when you're having fun. However, occasionally in hypnosis, you will find that time has been distorted in the other direction and feel that you have been in hypnosis for hours and hours when in fact only a few minutes have passed.

6. *Whatever Turns You On*

The next morning when I had finished my demonstration on pain management and the control of bleeding, I saw the doctor's beautiful wife go over to talk to the gentleman who had been my subject. As soon as I was free, I went over and joined them.

"Doctor Hunter, I could see this gentleman was smiling while you had him up here and he tells me he was having fun."

"It's great", he said. "You should try it!"

"I guess I forgot to mention that hypnosis is fun!" I said. "It's only heavy going when you're dealing with something difficult, perhaps something from the past. I think our friend here dissociated his arm — that is, he pretended his arm didn't belong to him — while I stuck the needle into him!"

He nodded. "That's right. It was a funny experience."

"That's why kids get a big kick out of hypnosis. They can ride on a magic carpet, become twelve feet tall, make their fingers and toes different colours — in other words, really experience the things that their imaginations stir up."

"Whatever turns you on?" asked the doctor's wife. "You don't mean to tell me that those people I saw on stage were having fun!"

"In their own way, yes."

Chapter Two

It's All In Your Head

Mrs. R's anxiety preceded her into my office. Her face was pale and her body was so tight that it seemed as if she was afraid it would break into little pieces if she loosened her control for a moment. She sat down across from me.

"I have a pain in my chest," she said.

"Show me where you get this pain."

She put her hand over her breastbone. "Right here."

"When did it begin? When do you first remember having this pain?"

"I was twenty-four *exactly*. It was my birthday."

I looked down at the form she had filled out for Marsha, my receptionist. Mrs. R. was forty-four now.

"Tell me about that first time."

"Well, my husband and I were in Winnipeg at a convention. It was so hot there, I remember. Then suddenly I got this awful pain. Just right out of the blue. I couldn't breathe, and it hurt so much that I couldn't move out of my seat."

"How long did it last?"

"Real bad? About an hour, I guess. Then it got easier and Ron took me back to the hotel."

"Did you take any medication? Did you see a doctor?"

"No. Ron got me a couple of aspirins and I went to bed."

That was the first occasion on which Mrs. R. had been aware of the pain, though she had the impression that it had happened to her before in a less dramatic way. Throughout the remainder of her twenties, she was plagued periodically by this pain.

Whenever it took over, she felt that it was possessing her, and she couldn't breathe.

When she was about thirty she began going to doctors for help. Each of them told her that her heart was fine, her lungs were fine, and that she must rest a little bit more and take things easy. Mrs. R., however, had three children, so it was difficult for her to take things easy and she simply carried on as before until the next bout of pain. This would probably have gone on indefinitely, but when she was thirty-seven, she was stricken with an attack severe enough to put her in hospital. There, she was investigated for ulcers, for a hiatus hernia, for gall bladder disease, and all the other things that doctors ordinarily think of in connection with a chest pain. Everything was normal. Her doctor sent her home to rest, but before he did, he introduced her to the word "psychosomatic" and it had been a red flag to her ever since.

In the two or three years before she arrived in my office she had seen eleven or twelve doctors. At least three of these were general practioners because she had shopped from one to another looking for help, and the rest were specialists of various sorts. She had asked for a referral to me when a friend had told her about hypnotherapy.

"And what did these doctors say about the cause of your pain?" I asked Mrs. R.

"They said it was psychosomatic," she said bitterly.

"And did they explain what that meant?" I asked.

She glared at me belligerently. "I know what it means! It means it's just in my head. That I'm imagining it!" Then before I could speak, she added furiously, "But this is *not* in my head! It's real! There's something really wrong with me. I'm not imagining it!"

"No, I'm sure you're not," I told her. "I believe you. *Your pain is real.*"

1. *Imaginary Versus Psychosomatic Illness*

Like many people, Mrs. R. believed that imaginary and psychosomatic meant the same thing, and my first task was to explain to her that although her pain was psychosomatic, it was not imaginary. The term "psychosomatic" comes from two Greek words — "psyche" which means mind or spirit, and "soma" which means body — and it was coined as a label for those illnesses which are the result of the interaction between mind and body.

Mrs. R. readily accepted the idea that certain illnesses belonged to this category. She understood that high pressured executives are more likely to have high blood pressure because she equated pressure on the job with pressure in the arteries. She even recalled commenting to a friend with high blood pressure that it was no wonder with the job he had.

She agreed that ulcers are psychosomatic because the emotional response of people under stress causes their stomachs to produce so much acid that it eats away at the lining of the stomach and the duodenum. She was even willing to agree that asthma is sometimes a psychosomatic illness because she knew of cases where an asthmatic attack had been prompted by emotional stress. Of course, she was also aware that allergies and infections contributed to these attacks, but she still recognized the important role of emotions in this.

I explained that ulcerative colitis also belonged in this category because it was caused by the individual's reaction to stress. Many kinds of arthritis, particularly rheumatoid arthritis, are also stress-related. Research in the last ten years has shown that rheumatoid arthritis patients are often people with a tremendous anger bottled up within them, and this finds expression in their red-hot angry joints.

But while all of these are acknowledged to be psychosomatic illnesses, they are also real illnesses because they can be measured or observed. For instance, everyone knows that high blood pressure can be measured on a blood pressure cuff. And no one denies the existence of ulcers because ulcers can be seen on an x-ray and because the patient can bleed to death with them. Pulmonary function tests on asthma patients will show that the actual intake of oxygen is drastically reduced and the small breathing passages (the bronchioles) are in spasm. Ulcerative colitis is a potentially catastrophic disease because the bowel is sometimes so badly eroded that the lower bowel must be removed. And rheumatoid arthritis causes such deformity and pain that no one could deny its reality. But all of these are psychosomatic because they involve an interaction between the mind and the body.

"But what about this pain in my chest?" said Mrs. R. impatiently. "None of those doctors have been able to measure what is wrong with *me*. They just tell me it's psychosomatic!"

"And you thought that they really meant it was all in your head. It's too bad that the word has developed such terrible connotations. Nowadays, the public thinks of people with psychosomatic illnesses as neurotics who are attempting to get attention or sympathy. Silly, frivolous people whose illnesses are not worthy of attention. There are even people who think it means malingering.

"Medical people have tried to escape these connotations by inventing euphemisms but many of their inventions are just as bad. Currently, the term "stress-related illness" seems to be the most acceptable.

"I believe *all illnesses are psychosomatic*," I told Mrs. R., "because they all involve an interaction between the mind and the body. If I develop a sudden severe pain, naturally I worry about it. I worry about its cause and its significance. That worry aggravates the pain, because I become more tense, my glands produce more adrenalin, my heart responds by palpitating, and I have difficulty getting my breath. It's a common — and logical — sequence of events. Did something of the sort happen to you?"

She nodded. "Yes," she said, "it was like that."

"And that's when you felt that you were being "possessed" by the pain."

"That's right," she said.

2. The Theory of Psychosomatic Disease

The Scandanavian Journal of Rheumatology Supplement* for 1975-77 contains a fascinating article on the theory of psychosomatic disease. Their surveys have shown:

> that personality structure and disease are inter-related, that repression of emotions causes both psychological and physiological regression, that inadequate and inconsistent facing of frustrations leads to organic dysfunction which in turn increases susceptibility to infection, and that behavioural patterns learned under environmental influences either enhance or inhibit susceptibility to disease.

Just ask a woman how her emotions affect her body and how her body affects her emotions during her monthly periods and she'll tell you all about it.

Until recently, nobody really knew how this process worked. But medical science, through a brand new branch called psycho-neuro-immunology, is finally discovering just how the mind and the central nervous system affect the body's response to disease and illness.

The keys to the process are neurotransmitters, chemical entities released by the brain to aid in the transmission of neural impulses. There are many of these neurotransmitters, but the one that we know most about is dopamine, a complicated molecule that acts as a chemical bridge for the impulse from one nerve to another. Now as a result of our knowledge of this molecule, doctors seeking to help people suffering the nervous tremor of Parkinson's disease can give them "methyldopa", a synthetic product with the properties of dopamine, and this medication forms the chemical bridge.

---

* The Scandinavian Journal of Rheumatology Supplement 1975-77, Supplement 18, page 11, Stockholm, 1977

Some of the neurotransmitters have a direct effect on the pituitary gland, the grand-daddy of the whole endocrine system. From it spring the hormones which will affect the thyroid and the adrenals and the ovaries and all the other endocrine glands of the body. The neurotransmitters that affect the pituitary come from the part of the brain known as the hypothalamus, the place where the emotional, intuitive, and feeling responses are processed. If you are happy and settled and doing well, the hypothalamus sends out neurotransmitters that pass on that message to the pituitary gland. But if you are anxious, upright, or under stress, the hypothalamus sends neurotransmitters with those warnings to the pituitary. If you are feeling positive about your abilities that's the message that's sent; if you are feeling negative, that's the story that goes out.

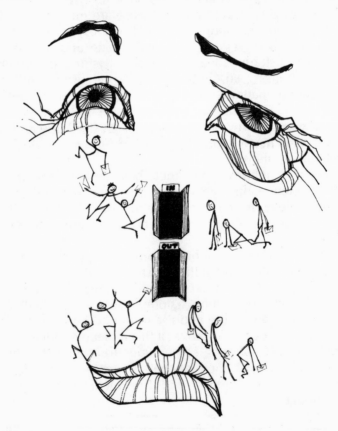

And there is a tremendous biofeedback mechanism at work here. For example, if you are anxious, your adrenal glands send forth adrenalin which has an effect on your whole body. The body sends on this anxiety message to the brain, and the brain passes on the message through the neurotransmitters. And round and around we go.

But the most important thing that has been discovered about neurotransmitters is that our whole bodies can be directly affected by our emotional intensity. Researchers have proved this in the lab by artificially synthesizing neurotransmitters and using them to stimulate the pituitary gland. We have a lot more to learn about the neurotransmitters, but we have no doubt now how they operate. And we know that because of their vital role in the basic functions of the body, we cannot separate our emotions from our physical responses.

Some emotional reactions seem to interfere with our physical function in only a minor way, but it may be that we are so used to our physical selves operating well that we don't recognize the positive influence of these emotions helping to maintain our good health. In fact, medical science is now beginning to recognize that many diseases occur when these positive emotions cease, that is, when the good things in our lives stop. In such cases, doctors now ask, "What good thing *stopped happening*?" instead of "What bad thing has happened?"

Certain kinds of cancer prompt this question. For more than a decade, we have known that the human body makes cancers all the time but that the body takes care of them. Science concluded from this that it was part of the normal cellular reproduction system and that it was being kept under control by some sort of magic barrier that they didn't yet understand. Only when the cancers escaped this control and multiplied beyond the body's capacity to deal with them are they labeled malignant. "But what," ask the doctors, "interferes with the natural protective mechanism that disposed of the cancers until that time? What made it stop?"

Research in this area may eventually show why certain types of cancer attack certain age groups, and why certain people have remissions and why others are completely cured. In the meantime, it is an important indicator of the value of the happy or positive emotions in the business of keeping well.

3. Psychosomatic Disease and You

"So the pain in my chest is caused by messages from my emotions," said Mrs. R. "That's a little different than saying that the pain is all in my head, isn't it?"

"It certainly is. Saying that it's all in your head means that it is imaginary. But your pain is real so the question is why are your neurotransmitters sending messages that cause you to react in this way. Sometimes," I went on, "it is virtually impossible to decide which came first, the physical illness or the emotional response, but I'm inclined to believe that some kind of stress always triggers the process. Maybe something that we're not aware of, or something that we don't identify as being particularly stressful. So we carry on for a long time under this stress, functioning in a perfectly normal way, then all of a sudden we get sick. It's sort of the-straw-that-broke-the-camel's-back type of situation."

Mrs. R. interrupted. "Are you saying that my pain may have started with something like Ron losing a big contract or my son getting into trouble at school?"

"Well, yes, but not that directly. Those situations are actually what medical science calls 'stressors'. In themselves they are neither good not bad, but inherent within them is a demand for change or action from you. How you *respond* to them is what we know as stress, and though we tend to think of stress as a negative thing, usually it is very positive."

In fact, if it were not for stress we wouldn't be alive at all because the very act of breathing is a stress reaction. For example, as air enters the lungs, the chest wall is stressed and therefore expands to accommodate the air intake. Similarly, every physical function — a heartbeat, a wave of peristaltic action — can be thought of as stress. If we do not have these reactions, these stresses, we have physical death. In the same way, we have a kind of emotional death if we have no stimulation or provocation of the emotional part of our lives. We see this in children who have been abandoned or have been used as scapegoats for their families. So we need stress to keep going.

Tension is somewhat different than stress but we need it to survive too. Though generally considered to be the same thing as stress, it is actually a separate factor on the health horizon. While stress involves a reaction, tension means that the body is held in a certain mode, that is, tense or taut. We use physical tension to stand upright or to walk; without it, we would collapse in a heap.

Emotional tension comes into the anticipation of some event or the concentration needed for working on a project. But although most tensions are really positive, only the negative ones seem to come to our attention. Thus we think of tension in terms of states of anxiety, of expectation, of waiting, of putting in time, of desperation. We say 'Harold is so tense, he's going to be sick!' when we mean that Harold's emotional balance is ready to crack. Sometimes, people deliberately make use of negative tension to keep a situation constant (for example the marriage that is welded together by hostility) because there is a certain kind of negative reward in it.

When a negative stress or tension is prolonged, an individual may react in one of three ways. First of all, he may identify the stress or tension, and use that knowledge to cope in more positive ways. This kind of person usually likes taking responsibility for his own well-being. On top of this, he may *need* to react positively because his image of himself is a positive one; he sees himself as a person who copes well and accomplishes things under adverse conditions or pressure. For example, he may need to set deadlines for himself to get his work done. I confess to writing my medical papers the day before I give them. Oh, I've been mulling them over for a long time before that, but I somehow need that deadline to get myself down to work. Like many people, I have a psychic need to show how capable I am and this seems to be one of my ways of proving it.

A second way to react to prolonged stress or tension is for the individual to feel miserable, refuse to or be unable to identify the source of the problem, and ignore possible solutions. He feels that everything is coming down on his head. "Why do all these bad things happen to me?" he asks as he settles into the victim's role. People in this category have a strong *negative need* to be punished or martyred. They get themselves into all kinds of stressful situations that they might have avoided if they had chosen to. They need to find out more about their emotional needs and understand the mechanisms by which they operate.

The third way to react to stress or tension is to get sick. That is, the body's physical response to emotional factors is illness. The people in this category do not get sick deliberately, they may even recognize the stress factors to which they are responding, but these factors are sufficient to cause them to become ill. They may get an ulcer, they may get tension tummy or a pain in the chest, or they may succumb to a virus.

Illnesses related to stress and tension are not limited to people who live high on the hog in North American society. Of course, if you have chosen to live the "simple life" and are happy doing so, you will probably avoid stress related illnesses, but the simple life is no guarantee of immunity. In the country district of central Kenya where I worked, young adults in the fifteen to forty bracket had begun to have rheumatoid arthritis and high blood pressure. They came in with anxiety symptoms, complaining, "Doctor, I am thinking too much!" They did not have enough education to secure jobs in their newly evolving country, but they had too much education to go back to the shamba and live in the old tribal way. "What am I going to do?" they asked. "I can't go back to the shamba. After all, I've been to school! What would they think of me?"

These Kenyans were striving for they know not what, just like the executive in Toronto who is not sure that he's got what he wants. It's a case of relative stress. Each suffers from anxiety to pull the thing off, to stay up on the heap. *Can I stay up here? What can I do for an encore? If I stay up here, I must have a big house and all the other accoutrements.* A little success breeds the need for greater success. Big success breeds fear of failure and fear of more success. And all this stress breeds ulcers and high blood pressure and arthritis and a hundred other physical responses.

"So I'll have to figure out what started it all, won't I?" asked Mrs. R. "But how will I do that? After all, it started so long ago!"

"Well," I said, "that's why you're here, isn't it? Let's get on with your hypnotherapy."

Chapter Three

Taking Responsibility for Your Health

Once we understand neurotransmitters and some of the mechanisms by which brain function can influence body response, and we recognize the role that stress plays in this sequence, the next step is to learn to *control* our emotional responses so that we can control our body reactions. We know that it is possible to control anger; we do this on almost a daily basis: generally we don't fly off the handle at the boss. We can learn ways of controlling fear and panic; we can even devise strategies for dealing with depression. So we can also put our minds to controlling other kinds of emotional response, particularly the kind that trigger physical illness.

When we learn to do this, we can truly assume responsibility for our own good health. There are no blanket rules for taking on this job because each person's body responds to its own particular emotional set. Each person reacts to stress in his own way, and under certain kinds of stress, each is more vulnerable to illness. That is, his physical body reflects what is going on in his emotional sphere in a manner typical of him.

This is why not all executives get ulcers. And not all housewives develop arthritis. Things that cause ulcers in one person don't cause ulcers in another person. Each individual responds in an individual way to stress, his neurotransmitters send out the appropriate messages, and his physical self responds in a typical way.

By becoming more and more aware of how your own *psyche* and your own *soma* work, you can do more and more to cut down the risk of illness and build up a positive attitude toward good health. You begin to recognize some facts about yourself that seem obvious when you discover them but have gone unrecognized when you weren't looking for them. If you know your own emotional set and your body's response, you can learn to take fewer risks with your health, but when you have to take a risk, you can do it in a commonsense way. In other words, if you have to go out in a canoe at midnight, make sure that you're wearing a life-jacket!

1. Getting to Know Yourself

When you decide that you want to take responsibility for your own health, the first thing you must do is identify the stresses and tensions that are hanging over you. Isolate them from the whole scene and identify them. This is not always easy because people tend to think of stress and tension as being caused by other people, whereas they are really the result of our *responses* to other people. And though we are not always responsible for what happens to us, we *are always responsible for how we* **respond** to what happens to us.

One of the most helpful things you can do to identify stresses and tensions is to get an outside opinion. Go to a counsellor, someone trained, who can look at your situation from a non-involved point of view. Some of the factors in this situation will be big and complicated, some will be small and nitty-gritty and day-to-day. But all are potential influences for illness or health, so it is necessary to identify them all.

Once you are aware of all these factors, it is time to make some intelligent choices. What are you going to do about them? This is a big part of the process of taking responsibility.

What are the choices? Can you improve the situation or should you quit the situation? Is it time to make a change or is it enough to understand what the stresses and tensions are so that you can learn to react to them less destructively?

This is the time to investigate your inner resources and learn how to use them. All of us have greater resources than we realize, but we only discover them in time of real peril. A soldier in the thick of battle will accomplish incredible things, feats that he would have never considered doing under ordinary circumstances. Mothers find they have superhuman resources when their children are in danger. To a less spectacular degree, however, we all dig into our inner resources every day to deal with the extra pressures in our lives. We line up too many appointments in the day but somehow we see to all of them. We promise more than we can possibly accomplish, but we do accomplish it. "Well, by gosh," we say, "I didn't think I'd get through all that, but here I am!"

People need to learn how to recognize these inner reserves and then how to make use of them once they have become aware of them. Some people use these reserves on an almost daily basis because they see themselves as the kind of person who can do everything, and do it exceptionally well and right on time. This self-image demands that they find the inner reserves to accomplish everything that they set out to do. Of course, if for some reason, they can't fulfill their expectations for themselves, one of the ways they can justify their "failure" is to get sick. Then they say, "No wonder I couldn't do it! Looking back now, I realize I had been feeling crummy for several days, but I had so much to do that I never paid any attention!" On the other hand, a person whose image of himself is that of someone who is incapable of doing anything right has probably never investigated his inner resources.

The safest image to hold as far as your health is concerned is that of a person with a reasonable expectation of being able to cope with most of life's problems as they arise. This is a person with enough gumption to see himself through day-to-day events and with enough inner reserves to deal with the unexpected. He has a sensible, appropriate self-image that is free of the stress of over-expectation or the dilemna of negative expectations. This kind of person feels comfortable about getting help from outside resources when he needs it. *There's nothing wrong with getting help.*

Another area that you can investigate in this business of taking responsibility for your own health is your family medical history and the role it can play in your own health. If your father and your uncle and your grandfather and three of his sisters and your great grandfather all had heart disease, there is a pretty fair chance that you are a risk! So you do the commonsense things: you eat conservatively, you don't smoke, you get regular exercise, you use alcohol in moderation. This is paying reasonable but responsible attention to family history. And having done that, you take a positive attitude toward the fact that you are going to control the situation to the very best of your ability, and that you don't intend to fall into the family history quagmire. Just because they all had it does not mean that you have to have it.

There does seem to be a familial tendency to grow cancers. That is, some families seem to be cancer-ridden while others seem to have a limited history of it. It could have something to do with the biochemical make-up of the members of the family, it could have to do with the area in which they were born and raised, or it could have to do with expectations. That is, not that the cancer itself was hereditary but that the tendency for the body to respond in that way was common to the members of the family. Therefore, given any encouragement at all, cancer will develop in these people.

Diabetes has a very positive family history; if your mother was diabetic, you may be a significant risk. The key here is the age at which she developed diabetes: if she became a diabetic at eighty, you have little risk but if she became diabetic at forty, your risk is considerably greater. There is an actual genetic factor in diabetes, so that it is in fact hereditary, but this does not mean you have to get it; it only means that you are prone to developing it. You can minimize your risk by watching your diet carefully and keeping your weight in check.

These are all positive ways that you can make use of your knowledge of your family's medical history. The people who really worry me are the ones who believe that their family medical history provides the blueprint for their own response to stress. The young woman who gets dysmenorrhoea (painful menstrual periods) and announces, "Of course, my mother had it too, you know." Or the woman who came to me complaining of migraine headaches (which they were not). "I don't understand it!" she said. "My mother never had migraines!" She was consoled however, with the fact that her twenty-year-old daughter was just beginning to get them! A tradition at last!

Responsible people are also aware of the possibility of making their worst predictions come true, fulfilling their own prophecies. "If I keep this up," they say, "I'm going to make myself sick!" And they do *both*: they keep it up and they get sick. Mothers and grandmothers are great for doing this to their children. They announce within the child's hearing, "If that kid keeps up like that, he's going to make himself sick!" And the kid does!

Our expectations for health and illness are very different today to what they were even twenty years ago. To-day we sometimes develop illnesses because our expectations are too high. Women suffer from this the most but men follow closely behind in the backsplash of the women's wave. Women are not allowed to be housewives anymore, although this used to be considered a most honourable profession. A woman is not allowed to be happy as a cashier in a restaurant; she must be planning for the next step up. But when these expectations are too much to cope with, the body accepts illness as a way out.

Twenty years ago, we didn't expect to be sick with the flu for more than two days. Today, patients come to me asking, "How long am I going to be sick, doctor? I've got a friend who's been sick with this bug for six months. Am I going to be sick that long?" And it is true that we have built bigger and better viruses today. With the best of intentions in the world, doctors tried to treat everything with antibiotics when they first came out, thereby doing two things: they changed the public's expectations of how to deal with illness, and they killed off all the good bugs which ordinarily keep the balance of nature. But they couldn't kill off the viruses because they don't react to antibiotics, so now we have tougher viruses to deal with, and people have learned to expect longer and tougher illnesses.

These expectations provide plenty of negative feedback, but

they also allow a lot of opportunities for positive intervention by the individual who really wants to fight back. The responsible person gets his expectations into line with reality, allowing them to relax a little so that they reach a level where he can be comfortable with them. He investigates stress-induced illness and looks over the factors in his own life which could pave the way to illness. And if he does get sick, he accepts that his illness may have a message about his lifestyle.

2. Taking the Blame

The concept of *taking responsibility for your own health is very different* to the concept of *taking the blame for getting sick*, because the implication of the latter is that you can get sick if you want to get sick. That is, people deliberately bring illness on themselves, repeatedly and consciously making themselves ill. Thus the patient is the victim of his own negligence or of his own emotional responses.

Some people take this idea of blame one step further and suggest that the patient is allowing others to victimize him. This is the concept of "being done to". The implication here is that someone else caused the patient's difficulties, that it was someone else's fault. Remember, we are not always responsible for what happens to us, but *WE ARE ALWAYS RESPONSIBLE FOR HOW WE RESPOND TO WHAT HAPPENS*, and this is where personal responsibility comes in. We can be the victor — the one who does the "doing" — when we are responsible for our own health.

Victimization is really far more sinister than simple blame because it means that the individual needs to be a victim, that somehow he has invited victimization. And while it is true that illness may fulfill a psychic need, a need to be punished, a need to be martyred, or a need to manipulate or hold control over someone else, I believe such drives are seldom conscious. More often, we find people feel so bad about themselves that they believe they should be punished, though in a much less obvious way. They might allow little derogatory things to happen to themselves such as the woman who allows her husband to talk down to her in public and who then explains that he has to have someone to do that to. Something in this woman's past forces her to believe that she must be treated in this way to make up for the wrong she thinks she has done, perhaps in her childhood. Certainly we

know that many children blame themselves for their parents' divorce, or their mother's death, or their father's heart attack, and they grow up looking for punishment.

For such people, the alternative to some kind of emotional or physical punishment is illness. If no one will punish you as you feel you deserve, you can punish yourself by being ill. This is terribly sad to see, especially where the individual does not remember or recognize the thing for which he is trying to atone. Fortunately, this is *not* common.

Secondary gain is sometimes the cause of illness, though it is more often the reason why the patient does not get well. The woman who has a very busy executive-husband gets no attention from him whatsoever until she gets sick, so she has relapses quite frequently. The man who has difficulty with exams gets headaches just before he is due to write each one. He is given permission to write later or to write his exam in a separate room; this allows him some control over the situation. Or perhaps he is forced to write it and fails; he then has an excuse for his failure.

These people are consciously using illness for secondary gain, although they do not consciously recognize this, because people have a fantastic capacity not to recognize what is blatantly obvious to other people.

A young woman involved in a motor vehicle accident continues to have pain three years later, and as a result, her insurance claim cannot be settled. She is not pretending or malingering although there is nothing physically wrong with her anymore. The pain is still real because the accident remains immediate and she is still caught up in the machinery of it. Her lawyer has asked me if she would get better faster if her court case was resolved and my answer has to be yes. She will improve faster when the accident and the court case cease to intrude too intimately into her day-to day life.

Until the last fifty years, it was not uncommon for women especially to suffer from "delicate health", a condition which allowed them to be the centre of the family's attention. Such women had very few ailments that you could actually name; there was just a vague ambiguous delicacy.

We mustn't upset Mama because her health is so delicate!
What's the matter with her?
Well, the doctors have never been able to find out!

In the old days women's opportunities were limited, but nowadays they can go out and compete: be a bank manager or a ski champion. In spite of this, doctors still meet patients who reel off the same kinds of symptoms. They have seen eighteen doctors and had five thousand tests, and it is the fault of the medical establishment that they haven't been cured. However, if some doctor did "cure" them, they would have to find some other way to be the centre of attention.

But none of these people — the ones who are seeking punishment or the ones who are seeking attention — are deliberately doing this to themselves. *They are not blameworthy.* They do not realize the mechanism for illness and they do not realize the possibilities for getting well.

There are, of course, practices which we know will cause illness. Smoking can cause lung cancer. Women who smoke and take birth control pills are at a very high risk for cardio-vascular disease. People who are obese are at a greater risk for diabetes, heart disease, and various degenerative diseases such as gall stones and arthritis of the knees. We know that people who drink alcohol are liable to get cirrhosis of the liver and pickle their brains.

And yet we also know that many people who have the intellectual capacity to understand these things still take pills, still continue to smoke, still carry far too much weight, and many of them do this in spite of a family history of heart disease or the knowledge that they already have too much sugar in their blood. And these people are perhaps the only group who have consciously refused to take responsibility for their own health.

But even when we are consciously aware of what we need to do to improve and maintain optimum health, we are not "home-free". Many people who come to me with this kind of problem tell me, "I know what I should be doing, but I just don't do it. I guess I have no willpower."

The truth is that they need to find out about the subconscious aspects of what they are doing and here is where self-hypnosis can give them insight.

Chapter Four

Self-Hypnosis and Every Day Living

The people who come to me for hypnotherapy or to learn self-hypnosis can be roughly divided into three groups.

First, there are those who are desperate for relief from their troubles. They have tried everything else and now, hoping to find a magic cure, they are willing to "try hypnosis."

Second are those whose symptoms are presently controlled by medication but who are rebelling against filling their bodies with chemicals. They are looking for ways to lessen their dependence on medication and increase their reliance on their own resources.

Third are the people who are neither desperate nor tied to medication. These are the people who are seeking a better pattern for their lives, a formula that they can use to organize themselves in a more useful and satisfying way.

It is difficult to help the people in the first group because *hypnosis is not magic*. It is the controlled use of one of the body's own natural mechanisms, but mastery of this control requires commitment and regular input on the part of the subject if it is to provide the longed-for relief.

The people in groups two and three have usually taken the first and hardest step toward assuming responsibility for their own health. They are quite willing to earn their good health by being aware, by being open to new ideas and possibilities and suggestions, by realizing that humans are not omnipotent and do not necessarily know all that they need to know about themselves, and by accepting the responsibility for seeking help when they need it. And that is why self-hypnosis is right for them.

Self-hypnosis will help them to take care of their bodies on a day-to-day basis, it will help them to deal with the little ailments that don't really require the ministrations of a doctor, and it will help them to deal with the ordinary stresses of life in a more productive way. It is the natural, do-it-yourself way to better health.

Unfortunately, although it should be an intuitive technique — as natural as falling in love — modern man has to take lessons in self-hypnosis because he has gradually concentrated most of his brain activity on thinking instead of giving equal time to his non-thinking capabilities. But thinking was never intended to be the primary function of the brain. Just look at prehistoric man for proof of this; the cortical or language and logic part of his brain was pea-sized while the limbic system, the part responsible for the maintenance of all the body functions, was enormous. This limbic system maintains homeostasis, the fine balance between the physical and emotional and mental functions of the body. However, as man developed through the millenia, the thinking brain grew larger and more complex while the non-thinking brain shrank. This doesn't mean that it became less complex; in fact, as it became more compact, it became more efficient in carrying out the emotional or spiritual or "subconscious" functions. But man had fallen in love with thinking and after he had ignored his non-thinking capacities for a few thousands of years, he lost the knack of using many of them.

1. Time Out for Hypnosis

I begin my self-hypnosis clinics by telling my students that they must take time to practice their hypnosis *every day* if they wish it to be really effective, but very often they wail, "I can't afford that much time!" This is balderdash. *Everyone has five or ten minutes a day to spend on better health!*

You can do your hypnosis while you are in the bathtub, or just before you fall asleep. Or you can set your alarm to wake yourself five minutes early. Or you can do it between shaving and breakfast.

Mother can take five minutes after the kids have gone to school, making it part of the day's routine, just like washing the dishes or vacuuming the floor. A new mother can do it after she's nursed her baby and he's fallen asleep. An office worker can do it before he leaves the office for home. (He'll probably get home faster anyhow because he'll miss the rush by ten minutes.) Or he can do it on the bus where no one will notice if he closes his eyes for a while. Or maybe it would not be out of line in the staff lounge to take a five minute "nap".

If you truly cannot find five minutes in your day for something so important as your health, then it is time to re-examine your priorities, because you are saying in effect that you are not an important person, and that you don't deserve time for yourself. *Regular hypnosis can help you re-establish the fact of your own importance.*

For the housewife, getting her hypnosis done each day should be as important as getting her dishes done. If the dishes aren't done, her family will have nothing to eat off; if her hypnosis doesn't get done she will have lost the opportunity to find out more about herself and to work on her problems from a different vantage point. And if she loses these things, her family is also the loser, and the loss will be infinitely greater than just having to eat off paper plates.

None of this emphasis on a regular time and place for hypnosis means that you can't do it at other times as well. Whenever you have need of the relaxation or insight that hypnosis can bring you, snatch thirty seconds or two minutes or six minutes and indulge yourself. Just remember to keep up your regular practice as well for your continuing homeostasis. And once you've found a comfortable way to induce your own hypnosis, you will be ready to use some or all of the following techniques to make it more useful to you.

1. USE AFFIRMATIONS

"Every day in every way I'm getting better and better. Every day in every way I'm getting better and better. Every day in every way I'm...."

There was a lot of sense to the repetition of this old maxim because it is a positive statement of progress. It is a reminder to yourself of the good things you are doing for yourself. It is an *affirmation*, but it will have more power with hypnosis, because an affirmation that reminds your *subconscious* of the progress you are making helps to maintain that progress even when you are not consciously thinking about it. If you are breaking a smoking habit, you can say, "soon I will be free from cigarettes!" If you are a reforming nail-biter you can say, "I am so glad that my nails are growing!" You will be delighted to see how soon this will be true.

2. BE POSITIVE

Remember that the subconscious mind does not hear negatives. When you tell yourself in hypnosis, "Now I'm not going to worry about this," the information you are giving your subconscious is, "Now I'm ... going to worry about this." Therefore, you must change this into a positive statement. "I'm going to think positively about this," or "I'm going to find a new way of coping with this." Ask your subconscious in hypnosis to let you know when you are making negative statements, whether overtly or implicitly, and then take the time to turn them into positive statements that your subconscious can use.

Be aware that when you say that you are "trying to" quit smoking or lose weight, that you are already admitting to possible or even probable failure. Count how many times you say, "Yes, but ..." "Yes, it's certainly a good idea, but it will have to wait until I have more time." You may kid yourself that this is just a delayed positive but it is really very negative. It doesn't take much effort to turn the idea around and say, "I have very little time and this idea seems very big and complicated, so I will find one aspect of it that I can start working on." *Even a small beginning is still a beginning.*

3. CONVERT NEGATIVE ENERGY INTO POSITIVE ENERGY

When people find themselves in a stressful or anxious situation, they send out waves of wasted energy. Negative energy. Energy which accomplishes nothing at all. Blaming yourself for things that are going wrong is also negative energy. You can convert this energy to positive use by concentrating in hypnosis on a situation where you might easily be self-accusatory or blaming, and experience that situation until you are aware of all the elements of your reaction to it. Follow this up with experiencing a positive situation and then compare the elements of both reactions. You will find that one of the elements that is common to both reactions is the flow of adrenalin, and the body's response to the flow. You will recognize the fluttery, geared up feeling and the need to go out and get involved in some activity right that minute. Since all the other elements of these reactions are really identical, it is just a matter of saying to your subconscious, "From now on, I want you to divert my energy positively instead of wasting it negatively."

Although this concept sounds a little nebulous when we deal with it with our conscious minds, when we think about it in hypnosis or have it presented to us in hypnotherapy, the subconscious invariably recognizes it as something that we can work on. The subconscious sees the significance of the similarities between the two kinds of reaction and puts the concept to good use.

4. OPEN UP TO NEW PERSPECTIVES

A small child looks at the house he lives in and it seems very big, the tree in the front yard is very tall, and the hill behind the house is very steep. But when the child grows to adulthood and goes back to look at that house, it seems to be just an ordinary sized house with an ordinary sized tree, and the hill behind the house has been reduced somehow to a gentler slope. Of course, the house and the hill and the tree have not changed. The person has. The important thing to realize is that both perspectives are right, but they are different because the situation of the person viewing them is different.

You can apply this idea to re-examining some of the situations in your own life where your thinking has become outdated. You need an opportunity to bring it up to date and to re-examine it from to-day's perspective. What stops many people from making this re-examination is the fear that if they change their minds now, they will appear to have been very stupid before. However, to-day's perception in no way diminishes an earlier perception. Both are right, but different because the person is different. At that time the individual saw it that way because that was the kind of situation he was in, but now he is in a new situation he deserves the opportunity to re-assess his perspectives. And hypnosis is oftentimes the medium through which the individual learns that it is all right to hold a different point of view than he held twenty years earlier.

5. ASSESS YOUR PRIORITIES

You can use hypnosis to help you decide whether to keep on doing what you are doing or do something new. One method of accomplishing this is a device I call "The Weigh-In", which involves weighing out the pros and cons of decision-making with a double set of scales.

Mary-Lou has a good job with a stock brokerage firm but is trying to decide whether she should stay there. The impetus for making a decision at this time is the fact that she has just broken up with her boyfriend who is also employed by the same company. In hypnosis, with her first set of scales, Mary-Lou has to decide whether to stay with or leave her present employer. On the one side of the scales, she puts all the things in favour of staying with her job, on the other side the things in favour of leaving:

For Staying In Job
Six years seniority
Knows her job thoroughly
Does her job well
Feels competent
Appreciated by her boss
Good salary
Good perks

For Leaving Job
Getting bored with routine
Looking to new adventure
Needs challenge
Wants more money
Difficult working with old beau
No interesting men in office

In hypnosis, Mary-Lou lets the scales strike a balance. This is her subconscious making an intuitive decision without interference from the thinking self.

Her second set of scales concerns an ad that she has seen in the newspaper for a cruise ship social convenor, so she loads these scales with the things in favour of this new opportunity on one side and with the things against it on the other.

In Favour of New Job
Travel perks
Probably good salary
New career direction
Opportunity for new mode of self-expression
Escape difficult beau situation

Against New Job
Fear of coping with new tasks
Job may not be compatible
May not be lucrative
May not enjoy coping with public
Unknown employee relationships
Probability of homesickness
Might miss opportunity to make up with boyfriend

When these scales strike a balance, Mary-Lou is ready to weigh the heaviest side of this scale against the heaviest side of the first scale. This final balance should tell her:

a. Do I really need to make any change at all?

and   b. What change should I make if I do need a change?

Mary-Lou may end up not following the dictates of the scale, but she will be able to live comfortably with that decision because she has explored the problem with her subconscious and knows all the elements of it. Perhaps in the end it will be her conscious mind which overrides the balance struck by the scales; she may re-assess the situation at a later date.

Another way to assess your priorities is to differentiate between the behaviour patterns imposed upon you by other people and the behaviour that is really part of you as a person. We are all very prone to pay attention to the "shoulds" that come from outside ourselves, especially the ones that come from friends and family. It is very easy to accept their standards, their sense of duty, and their moral obligations, but even as we accept them, we rail against them. We need to find out what is really appropriate for us in our dealings with the world.

In hypnosis, we can discover which of the "shoulds" are appropriate. The ones that we are ranting and raving against are not for us because they are not part of how we really see the world. They come from outside of ourselves so we should consider them from a very objective point of view; we should think of them as *accessory information*. Maybe they are valid for someone else but not for us; we can keep them in mind but we don't have to pattern our lives on them.

When we reject the standards that others impose on us, we are likely to stir up hostility because people tend to feel that what is good enough for themselves is good enough for everyone else. This is the hardest part of making such choices. Suppose, for example, that your mother has given you advice about raising your children. You don't agree with her but you think: if I don't do it her way, mother is going to be hurt! Meanwhile, your subconscious is saying: if I don't do this mother's way, she is going to make life unbearable for me! In fact, it isn't really a matter of keeping mother content; it is a matter to keeping down mother's hostility.

Sometimes, after coming to grips with this in hypnosis, you can deal with the situation by talking it over with the offended person. You can make a simple statement of fact: "Mother, I don't want to bring up my children that way." Some people deal with the problem by never referring directly to it, but carrying on as their own "shoulds" tell them to. But once you realize the validity of your own "shoulds", you have at least been given the freedom of choice.

6. WEAR SOMEBODY ELSE'S SHOES

There are times when I know that I — like most people — am better at seeing other people's problems clearly than I am at seeing my own. For them, I can help because I am outside the problem and can bring the perspective that comes with objectivity; for myself, it is more difficult.

To get around this, I sometimes go into hypnosis and pretend that I have a patient named Marlene who has this particular problem. Usually, I know perfectly well what I would suggest to another person in a similar situation, so I need a vehicle through which I can say it to myself. Doing it on a conscious, logical, intellectual basis does not work, as my emotions continue to throw in endless "YES, BUTs!"

In hypnosis, I am a little more likely to consider alternatives that I otherwise might reject because of background, because of emotional factors, because of my reluctance to get away from a safe or familiar way of doing things. Hypnosis allows me to wear someone else's shoes and play the role of counsellor as well as the role of client. Once I can begin to accept the concept in hypnosis, then I can go on to work through the details in the usual logical way.

7. FIND THE ELEMENTS OF YOUR PROBLEM

Sometimes it is helpful to apply a very artificial formula to a situation that has you baffled. The value of applying a formula to it is that it isn't going to fit exactly. You're going to have to bend the situation to fit and when you bend things they are apt to crack a little, and even the smallest crack may provide you with an opening to attack the problem.

"Dr. Hunter's Three Little Boxes" formula allows you to divide up all the component parts of your problem into *three separate boxes*. The first box which you create in your subconscious has a big label reading: OTHER PEOPLE. Into it you put all the parts of your problem that have been brought to it by other people. *You do not put the people themselves into the box*, just their contributions to the problem. For example, part of Anna's problem is the fact that her mother is hurt by what Anna is doing, so mother's hurt should go into the box. Mother should not go in.

The second box is labelled: FACTS; it is simply for the facts of the situation. If you have a deadline to meet, then the date of the deadline goes into the box. Perhaps even the fact that a deadline exists at all belongs in the box as well. Milton, who will soon be sixty-five, is concerned about being forced to retire. Since his age is a fact he cannot change, it goes into this second box.

The third box is for the parts of the problem which you contributed yourself. It is labelled: ME. Most of the things in this box will be your reactions to events, things like fear, pride and anger. Perhaps you want to take a job in another city but the last time you decided to do this your mother had a heart attack. Your resentment and fear go into box three.

When all the components of your problem have found homes in one of the three boxes, you pick up the first box, full of other people's contributions to your problem, and *you throw it away*. You cannot change anything that other people contribute so there's no sense worrying about it; that's their problem, not yours. But make sure you haven't put any of the people themselves into the box before you throw it away. You can't afford to get rid of them; they're far too important to you.

Pick up the second box, the one full of facts, and heave it out, too. You can't change anything in this box either. Certainly the situation may change in time and you'll have a whole new set of facts to assess, but right now these are the facts and you can't change facts. There's no sense wasting energy on things that you cannot change.

Now if you take a look at the problem after you've thrown those two boxes away, invariably it will seem different. And it *is* different. *Furthermore the parts of it that are left are the parts that you have some chance of doing something about.* You are now in a situation where you can do something rather than have everything done to you.

And right now while you are feeling good about having reduced the problem is a good time to have a closer look at the contents of that third box, the one full of your own contributions. There may be and almost surely will be some things that you bring to the problem that for some reason you don't want to change. It doesn't even matter what your reasons are or whether they are selfish or trivial. If you are not ready to do anything about changing them right now, all you have to do is recognize these feelings, so that you can put them away someplace where they are accessible. When you are ready, you can take them out and re-assess them.

Perhaps you are in a difficult situation with your best friend. What she has done makes you feel bad, and you are not yet ready to give up feeling bad about it. You are not finished with that emotion, so for now you can put that feeling away.

Perhaps there are also things in this last box that you truly *cannot* change even if you wanted to. These can be put into a separate little box and shipped out after the first two boxes. There is no point in frittering away your time, energy and resources on things you cannot change.

So at last you are left with very few parts of the original problem, usually just one or two components that you brought to the situation and that you are willing to chance. *And that's where real problem solving begins.* Let yourself find some small part of the problem — the smaller the better — so that you can make a start with a very, very little shift in your life. Anything that shifts and changes even the slightest bit means that everything else around has to shift and change to accommodate it. Therefore as soon as you've made the first move, you have begun the resolution of the problem. You're on your way. And from there on, it will proceed at your own pace.

8. TAKE TIME FOR A DAYDREAM

Sometimes your best use of self-hypnosis is to enjoy a ten-minute daydream while your subconscious works on your problems. Enjoy a trip to Fiji, or a ski holiday in the Laurentians, or a vacation in Disneyland. You will come out of hypnosis feeling fresh and relaxed with the added bonus of knowing that your subconscious has been quietly getting on with the job.

Chapter Five

Sound The Alarm

1. Can you give me something for this cold, doctor?

Even after you have accepted the responsibility for your own health, there may be times when you get sick. You may have let some factors slide by without clueing in to them or recognizing them, or perhaps understanding their potential influence. Or perhaps you didn't realize how stressed you were, or how much energy you were using up so that your body defences were at a low ebb.

When this happens, being a responsible person, you do the responsible thing. You take yourself off to a doctor to get some commonsense basic investigation done and to find out if there is some medication that you should be taking, just as you would go if you broke your arm or leg, because he is the only person with the expertise to set it for you. At times like this, your doctor has the knowledge and equipment to help you.

Unfortunately, patients who have assumed personal responsibility for their own health sometimes create a dilemma for both themselves and their doctors, as the experiences of Mrs. S. and Mrs. J. illustrate.

Mrs. S. is an intelligent forty-two year old woman who has been feeling less than well for about four months. Nothing really specific, but just not her usual vigorous, joyous self. She goes to see her doctor and tells him her symptoms. She feels run down, she says, and complains of sleeping poorly. It isn't that she can't fall asleep, but she wakes up off and on throughout the night so that when morning arrives, she feels she hasn't slept at all. Her periods have become unpredictable too, but everyone tells her that she has to expect this at her age. She's irritable and impatient with everybody and that's not like her. In the past she has always coped well under similar circumstances.

Her joints ache. One morning she wakes with her ankle paining and the next day it's her knee giving trouble. Her digestion is poor and her smoker's cough is worse than usual. But it was the three colds she had in the last two months which finally prompted her to visit her doctor.

"Can you just prescribe an antibiotic for my cold?" she asks him.

Now Dr. A. is a very conscientious physician who honestly cares about his patients. He does a careful physical on Mrs. S. and he finds that her blood pressure and her weight are both up a little. Because of her cough he sends her to have x-rays done on her chest, and because she is having digestion problems, he arranges for a "barium swallow" as well. She also has a cardiogram and a urinalysis. Blood tests show that her hemoglobin is down; she's a trifle on the anaemic side, nothing much but enough to make her feel draggy.

Dr. A. has treated Mrs. S. and her family for a long time so he knows the family problems. He knows, for instance, that Mr. S. is an executive who is out of the house from six in the morning until nine at night, and when he finally gets home he generally brings his problems home with him. He wants his wife to be waiting there for him to tend to his needs while he relaxes. Mrs. S. copes with most of her teenagers' problems by herself. Knowing all this, Dr. A. advises her to take a little iron for her hemoglobin, a diuretic for her blood pressure, and some tetracycline for her cold, even though he knows that antibiotics won't kill viruses. (He likes to give people the things that they ask for as he feels there is therapeutic value in that.)

He tells Mrs. S. that the x-rays for her chest and her stomach are negative, and he gives her a little Dalmane (a hypnotic) to make her sleep. Although he concedes that it is a bit early for her to have entered the menopause, she is obviously menopausal, so he gives her some Premarin which is an estrogen replacement. As for her general feeling of "blah-ness", he reassures her, she's just tired of coping with all these minor troubles. She'll feel better when she's got them under control. As she goes out the door, he hands her a diet sheet and then, because he *is* a conscientious doctor, he arranges for a follow-up appointment to re-check her hemoglobin and her blood pressure.

Dr. A.'s performance is very typical of the routine that doctors get into. They give a thorough examination, they treat the symptoms, they arrange for a follow-up. They care about their patients and although they don't spend much time talking to them, the talk they do give them is very reassuring.

Mrs. J. goes to Dr. B. with nearly the same set of symptoms. She is feeling run down, she hasn't been sleeping very well, her periods are irregular, she is irritable and impatient, and she gets a lot of vague aches and pains. She's had three colds in two months, she has a smoker's cough, and her digestion is a little upset. Dr. B.'s nurse has squeezed Mrs. J. into his appointment schedule because she just needs something for her cough.

Dr. B. is also a conscientious and caring physician and he recognizes that her problems may take a little longer than just "breathe in and breathe out" and away you go. He arranges for blood tests so that she won't think that she is just being dismissed, and he asks her to come back the next day for a longer appointment.

When she comes back, he does basically the same things that Dr. A. did for Mrs. S. He gives her a careful physical examination. He sends her for x-rays of the chest and then he sits down to talk about her problems. He prescribes a little iron for her hemoglobin but he also gives her some instruction in nutrition and how she could improve her diet so as to get more iron into it. "Then you won't have to go on taking an iron supplement forever," he tells her.

He then explains that her iron deficiency is probably a factor in the irregularity of her periods, but that her hormonal cycles, family upsets and other stresses are all interrelated. "Stress factors in your household can be affecting how your hormones respond to stress. So I think it's a little premature to be thinking about the menopause in your case. You may need a little Premarin later on, but I don't think it's appropriate at this point in your life."

Since she had asked for antibiotics for her cold, he takes time to explain that antibiotics don't work on viruses. They work well on bacteria because bacteria have independent metabolisms; the antibiotics simply interrupt the way the bacteria multiply or the way they form cell walls or the way they take in nutrition. But viruses don't have that independent mechanism. They are parasites which invade the host cell and live off it. So if you set out to interrupt the life cycle of a virus, you have to interrupt the life cycle of the host cell as well. Consequently, antibiotics have no effect on the viruses that cause colds.

Since Mrs. J.'s blood pressure is up, Dr. B. does consider a diuretic, but he also talks to her about some of the other things that she could do to bring her blood pressure down; perhaps she could start doing some yoga or meditation for relaxation, or begin regular exercise classes. He goes on to discuss exercise at some length, in fact, because her weight is up a little, and though exercise is not only, or even mainly, a weight reduction technique, he feels that she could use the general physical toning that it will provide as well.

He encourages her to stop smoking because smoking does not contribute to her general health, and he even tells her about a woman doctor he knows who conducts anti-smoking hypnosis clinics. He urges her to investigate life-style counselling to find other ways to reward herself instead of smoking. As far as her sleep patterns and irritability are concerned, he points out that these are common responses in stressful situations, and she should be reassured that the time will come when she will sleep easily again and be comfortable with her children again. He suggests some stress reduction techniques to help her to cope in the meantime.

The problems arise when Mrs. S. and Mrs. J. emerge from their doctors' offices. Mrs. S. has a purseful of prescriptions. She is dissatisfied with the whole medical profession. What she wanted was a better understanding of the mechanics of good health and how she could help herself toward it.

"Dr. A. is no good," she announces to anybody who will listen. "All he knows how to do is write a prescription! I'll bet he's getting a kickback from the drugstores!"

Actually, her condemnation is unjustified. Dr. A. is doing what he was taught to do in medical school, that is, assuming responsibility for his patients' health.

Meanwhile, Mrs. J., who believes that pharmaceutical companies were put on earth to gratify her specific needs, comes out of Dr. B.'s office declaring that he paid no attention whatsoever to her problems.

"He didn't even give me any medicine!" she cries in frustration.

Dr. B. believes his patients should share the responsibility for good health. When he hears of Mrs. J.'s complaints, he makes a mental note to find more roundabout ways of telling his patients that they don't need medication, that there are things they can do to help themselves to overcome illness, and that patients and doctors must be partners.

People who rely on their doctors to maintain their good health are abdicating their responsibility. After all, each individual is in a far better position to keep in touch with his own body than his doctor is! And just as no one else has the responsibility for making them happy in this life, no one else has the responsibility for keeping them healthy. Not spouses nor parents nor doctors. *The onus is on the individual to do as much as possible to maintain his own good health.*

Could Mrs. S. and Mrs. J. have avoided their trips to the doctor? No. Not after their symptoms had appeared. They both did the responsible thing then by going for help and advice. But perhaps at an earlier stage, before their symptoms had appeared, they could have avoided the trip if they had understood that something was *about to go wrong*, if they had recognized the alarm bell ringing in their subconscious and had known what steps to take to avoid illness.

2. Alarm Bells

Harry H. has held an executive position for many, many years with a large appliance manufacturing company. He is a highly organized man so a lot of work crosses his desk in the course of a day. And he runs a board meeting like a board meeting ought to be run.

But Harry has been finding himself more and more frustrated lately. Things are not going as he feels they should. He gets his work done but it's a real struggle. None of his assistants seem to be pulling his own weight so that he feels as if he is dragging them along, too. And to make things worse, no one seems to understand what he is saying anymore.

This state of affairs continues for some months before Harry gradually begins to realize that there is something physical about the state he is in. Looking back, he realizes that he has been tired for the past three months and maybe longer. He can hardly get out of bed in the morning and he is dragging himself through each day. At first, he is tempted to blame the situation in his office for his fatigue, but then he realizes: *No wonder things are going bad at the office! I'm tired out!*

Harry is elated to have defined the problem that was obstructing his personal production line. It's fatigue! *Therefore*, thinks Harry, *there must be a physical cause*, and he tells his secretary to make an appointment for him with Doctor B. Harry is now in an upward mood swing. A few pills and he'll be his old self again! *Darn good thing I realized what was giving me all this trouble*, he thinks as he trots off to see Doctor B.

The doctor takes a careful history, a complete physical and a number of relevant investigations: a cardiogram, some blood work, blood pressure and so on. All the tests come back within normal limits. His blood pressure is a little high but it always has been. He is a little overweight but that's not a new condition either. There is nothing physically wrong with Harry, in fact, that would account for the way he is feeling.

Harry leaves Doctor B's office feeling discouraged. He had really believed that he had the situation in hand, that all he needed was some professional help to put things right. Now he feels a little betrayed by the doctor. *He should have found something wrong or at least prescribed something*. He walks back into his office with nothing changed.

Now Harry's mood goes into a downward curve, but since he's an intelligent man, he is still churning the whole thing over in his mind. *There's got to be more to this,* he thinks. *When was it that I started to feel tired?* And little by little he remembers.

It was when his son Jim got into trouble. Harry had always figured that Jim was a good boy, and he had stuck by his son and gone to court with him, and when Jim was put on probation, Harry had done all the things that a supportive parent should do. But the whole thing had left him feeling inadequate as a parent. *Was it his fault that the boy got into trouble?* he asked himself. He had read about fathers who didn't give their kids enough time. His self-doubts churn around and around in his head, and even when he is in the thick of production quotas and export data, they hammer away at a corner of his brain.

Dimly, it dawns on Harry that his inner battle and his office responsibilities are taking an almost equal share of his energies and attention. He knows that he cannot afford to skimp on the energy he puts into his job, but he is equally aware that his personal war is leaving little energy for anything else. He goes back to see Doctor B. They talk over Jim's problems and Harry's reaction to them and how they have affected his health. Doctor B., who uses hypnotherapy in his practice, introduces hypnosis to Harry as a new means of communicating with his subconscious, and as a result, Harry begins to get a better understanding of himself as a person, and a reassurance that when Jim's difficulties occurred Harry did the best he could.

Harry's problems and their eventual resolution have followed a three part curve that is very typical of the reaction which responsible people — or at least those who are trying to be responsible — have when they are dealing with a health problem. Much as we would all like to comprehend the nature of our problems in a flash and undertake their solutions without aid, we are condemned to stumble through an emotional minefield just like Harry's before we come to the happy ending. But the journey can be much simpler for each of us if we can follow the road map and recognize the landmarks.

Harry's journey began when he heard an inner alarm telling him that something was wrong. Like most of us, he did not have time to call a halt in his life while he tended to the alarm. It came at an inconvenient time, but it was insistent. Nothing dramatic, just a little inner voice niggling, niggling, niggling until he finally paid attention. He was tired and as a result he was not coping with his job. Of course, for some of us, the alarm sounds in a much more dramatic way, and we have to drop what we are doing and resolve the problem right then and there, but this is rather rare. For most of us, the alarm is this still voice from our subconscious, telling us to wake up to the problem.

Harry's reaction to the alarm was elation. "Ah, now I know what's wrong," he said. But his elation was short-lived because it turned out that he really didn't know *what* he had pinpointed and he didn't know what to do about it. Harry went downhill then into a trough of despondency.

He became imprisoned in his situation. He knew he was too tired to carry out his job but he didn't know why he was tired or what he could do about it. He was in a worse position now than he was before he heard the alarm and went to see Doctor B. because Doctor B. had eliminated the easy solution that he had envisaged. However, sometimes when you find yourself locked into what appears to be a hopeless situation, you can choose to re-interpret the situation to make it useful instead of destructive. That is, instead of seeing your life in this prison as merely confining, you can appreciate it for being simpler. Not *easier* in any way, but *simpler*. You can say, "Okay, I'm in this prison. I can't do a lot of the things that I usually do because I have no choice. So *temporarily* I will accept this fact and put aside those things that will have to be dealt with when I get out of here." Harry, for example, simply could not cope with his job once he was in his trough of despondency, so he had to cut back on the things he was trying to accomplish. He simplified his life by delegating things to others and put all his energies into his necessary activities.

In this simplified lifestyle with all the frills swept clear, there was time and space to think, time for some real insight to germinate. When things are simpler, you are more likely to recognize insight when it begins to raise its head. It is this re-thinking that is so useful because this experience is going to be the basis for future behaviour.

Harry began to climb out of his prison and up the long curve toward physical health when he finally realized that his reaction to his son's troubles had a bearing on his present fatigue. His moment of insight marked the recognition of true responsibility for his own condition. He was ready to step out on a new pathway with more options than he had ever had before.

3. Alternatives

If you don't want to deal with the factors leading up to the crisis which set off your alarm bells, you can find other ways to escape the immediate problem.

1. You can manipulate the present situation to make it more manageable. This is rather like shaving off the corners of the pieces in a jigsaw puzzle; you can make them fit all right but what do you do when you find the correct piece to fit that hole?

When this system involves only yourself, it may work, but when you try to force someone else into the situation as well, it is bound to backfire. For example, Abigail and Richard were involved in a power struggle within their marriage, when the question of redecorating the long entrance hall in their home arose. Abigail loved the wallpaper that she had put up in the hall some years earlier. Richard hated it and said so repeatedly. Finally, Abigail decided to control the situation by stripping off the wallpaper she loved and demanding that Richard paint the hall. But once the wallpaper was off, Richard refused to paint the hall. Abigail's response was to pack up and leave home. Her method of manipulating the situation may have been all right for herself but Richard was not going to play by her rules.

Except for the fact that Abigail was an intelligent woman who came to her senses once she had distanced herself from the immediate situation, this marriage might have ended right there. Fortunately, she went home and with Richard's co-operation began examining the factors which led up to their problem.

2. Another way to deal with a conflict situation that has made you either psychologically or physically ill is to project all of the negatives of the situation out onto other people. Then by fighting these people, you need never come to grips with the real problem.

For those people who use this technique, it is very difficult, if not impossible to say, "I wonder what *my* role is in all this?" Instead they complain that everybody has conspired against them, or that the situation was stacked against them. Teenagers, for instance, who know they are behaving outrageously, sometimes ease their feelings by blaming their troubles on their families, thereby making the entire household miserable. Once they have chosen this method of dealing with their problems, everyone else in the family has to somehow adapt to their gameplan. Either they feed into the teenager's central role or opt out or stand on the periphery, but they cannot escape its effect. It is part of a power struggle, a shifting and adjusting of roles.

3. The third method of dealing with your problems is to refuse to acknowledge them and bury them as deep as you can. Well-meaning friends have a tendency to insist that we forget our troubles once they are over but this is very dangerous. Forgetting means burying, and the human organism cannot cope indefinitely with buried stress. Eventually it has to express itself.

We should instead, be allowing these past experiences — especially the soul-searing ones — to acquire a more comfortable perspective as we gather new knowledge. Re-interpreting can lead us to new ways of coping with stress and anxiety.

An example of this came in a very touching experience which I had not long ago. A man of forty-six was referred to me for hypnotherapy for his high blood pressure. In the course of taking his history, I asked how many brothers and sisters he had.

"None," he said, then corrected himself. "Well, I did have a sister but she was killed when she was five."

When I looked up from filling in my notes, he continued, "I was sixteen at the time. I'd just got my driver's license the week before. Mother said I was too young to drive, but she gave in finally and I got my license. Kathy wanted to buy flowers for Mom's birthday so I played the bigshot and took her to get them in the family car. When we came back, my Uncle Phil's car was in the driveway so I parked across the street from the house, and Kathy hopped out with the flowers and ran toward the house.

"A car hit her. She didn't even see it coming. When I got to her she just looked up at me, then closed her eyes and died. I couldn't believe it had happened. I just sat there in the street holding Kathy. She still had the bunch of flowers in her hand.

"Then Mother came out screaming. And you know what she screamed at me? She said, 'I knew you were too young to drive!'

My patient had told his story quite matter-of-factly but I realized that the words covered a depth of emotion that thirty years had not softened. In the discussion that followed, he told me how his mother had repeatedly accused him of being incapable of loving anyone because he had not cried over his sister's death. On a conscious level he had long ago convinced himself that he was a loving person and that he had not been responsible for Kathy's death, but he was still trying to make amends to his mother. As a parent now himself he was in a better position to understand the anguish his mother had felt, but in his mind's eye he could still see himself sitting in the street holding his dead sister, his grief and shock so great he could not cry, and his mother screaming at him.

This patient proved to be a very good hypnosis subject and we made good progress with his blood pressure problem. Consequently, I suggested one day that it was time we softened his early traumatic experience. In hypnosis I took him back thirty years to his mother's birthday and talked him through the event once again.

"Just imagine," I said, "that little girl, so happy with the flowers for her mother. She's running now across the street. She doesn't see the car so she's not scared at all. And when she is hit, she doesn't feel it because it happens so suddenly and the shock is so great. The only thing she knows is that her big brother is holding her in his arms, the brother she loves so much. And then she just closes her eyes and it is over.

"If your mother had understood how much you loved Kathy, she would have known that you had done all you could, wouldn't she?"

"But I didn't tell her. How could she know?" he said.

"And now that you are a parent yourself, you understand that when you are really worried, the words that you say are often not what you mean. And that your mother was *blaming herself* for allowing you to drive — even though that had nothing to do with the accident."

With this new insight, he understood both consciously and subconsciously that his mother had no way of knowing how he had felt and had no other way of expressing how she had felt. In the intervening years, he had learned how to interpret events more accurately, but only by going back and re-experiencing this event was he able to *apply* these present concepts to understanding the past.

How many times have you thought: "If I'd only known that at the time, I'd have done things differently." Frequently, when we look back on the problems we had in the past, we can redefine them in terms of our present understanding because we have acquired new information in the meantime. In hypnosis especially, it is possible to re-experience something from the past in the way *that you wish it had occurred.* This is a legitimate re-working of the event because in this way, you can go back and accept what happened then, while allowing yourself the privilege of knowing that you did your best at the time. Only in the light of your present knowledge could you have done better.

4. The last and best way to deal with the factors which set your alarm bells ringing is by following in Harry's footsteps. It's guaranteed to work but you must realize in advance that you may have to deal with a bunch of factors that you really did not want to think about, and if these factors are going to weigh you down then you may be saddled with another problem.

It's always much easier to say, "When all those terrible things happened to me what else could I do?" You can collect a good deal of sympathy and feel maligned and put-upon. It's difficult to look at the factors involved in your problem and say, "So that's why it happened! Well, I'd better get busy changing things!"

Here-and-now therapy that most psychiatrists and hypnotherapists subscribe to to-day is based on the idea that it is definitely worthwhile to find out about things in your past because it will help you to understand how you came to be in your present situation. But this therapy says that it is worse than useless to spend time worrying about something that you can't change. You must ask what you can do here-and-now to make things better.

The past has a different pattern from the present, a pattern that we can appreciate when we look back on it from the vantage point of the present. In travelling through life, we never arrive back at exactly the same place. As if we are travelling on a spiral, when we come back to the same place we have changed levels so we see it from a different angle, from a new vantage point. And we perceive it as if for the first time. In this way we learn from past experience and take responsibility for the future.

Chapter Six

Signs, Symptoms and Symbols

It was already 9:48 on a beautiful April morning when I parked my car in the reserved slot outside my office. I had delivered a baby boy at 6:30 that morning, done my hospital rounds, dealt with a lacerated knee in the emergency ward, and come out of the hospital to find that I'd left my headlights on and my battery was dead. As a result, by the time I entered my office, the waiting room was already full and I had a hunch that it was one of those days where I would never quite catch up.

Twenty-four year old Jerry C. was my second patient. I'd known him since his mother sent him to my office ten years earlier. He had acne then, and he still had it now.

"Look at me!" he fumed. "I look like some teenager!"

I examined his skin and, as he had some very deep lesions, I decided that a systemic antibiotic would be appropriate.

"This prescription will last you a week. Be sure to use the whole thing, and then let me have a look at you again." I signed the prescription and handed it to him.

"Thanks, Doctor Hunter," he said, and then with the door half open, he turned back. "Oh, by the way, this stuff won't upset my stomach, will it? I've been feeling kind of nauseated lately."

There was no reason why a healthy young man like Jerry should be feeling "kind of nauseated lately", so I knew that this was Jerry's way of introducing his real problem to me — a problem that was disturbing him as much and probably a lot more than the acne that he had supposedly come to see me about.

Every doctor has patients like Jerry. They are the people who wait until the end of the visit to casually mention their real concerns, because they are too frightened to bring them up at once. They toss them off in this offhand way hoping to make them sound unimportant because they are hoping against hope that they will turn out to be unimportant. Perhaps the doctor will even say, "Tell me about it next time", and then they may never have to talk about it at all. And lurking in the background of their carefully staged performance is the fear that the doctor will find the whole thing foolish or a waste of time. Having the door half open can turn this casual complaint into an exit line if the patient has to save face.

But every doctor knows that he must take some time to deal with such problems immediately because the patient needs support then and there. And it doesn't really matter that there are ten people sitting in the waiting room because this patient will have to come first. (And that is why, in spite of your doctor's good intentions, you will sometimes get a stern look from him after you have geared yourself up for a week to make this kind of a confession!)

My young friend Jerry obviously needed something more than an antibiotic for his acne, but without adequate investigation, I didn't know what that "something more" should be. And he needed an opportunity to talk his problems through.

"Can you come back tomorrow, Jerry?" I asked. "You and I need more time to work on this and I'd like to run some tests to see if we can pinpoint your stomach trouble."

"Sure," he said, and I could see he was relieved that I had not dismissed his plea for help.

The next day's examination showed nothing abnormal. Blood pressure normal. No lumps or bumps in the chest or abdominal area. No problems in the urinary tract. Barium swallow negative. Physically, Jerry was a normal, healthy young man. But he was still experiencing nausea.

"Well, there's no apparent physical reason for your trouble, Jerry...."

"Then what's the matter with me?"

I had known Jerry and his family long enough that I could ask blunt questions without giving offence, so I asked, "How are things at home?"

He shrugged, but it was obvious he knew what I was getting at. "You think this is emotional?" he asked.

"It might be worth looking for stress factors that are contributing to your trouble."

"Okay," he said at last. Then he grinned. "Does this mean I get some of your famous hypnotherapy, Doctor Hunter?" His mother had used hypnosis for her insominia and he knew it worked.

"You took the words right out of my mouth," I told him.

Jerry learned hypnosis quickly, and consequently, at the second session when his breathing had become slow and steady and his body was relaxed, I decided that he was in a suitable level of hypnosis to use role-playing with him. Using ideas which I had gleaned from his mother's most recent visit to my office, I played the role of his mother and nagged Jerry about the junk food that he ate, the hours he was keeping, and how his father and I never saw him anymore.

"You only come home to eat and sleep," I told him.

Suddenly his breathing pattern changed and he burst out in exasperation, "You make me sick! Leave me alone!"

And what he said was literally true. The anger and frustration that he had not expressed to his mother, but had just expressed to me in hypnosis was actually making his nauseous.

1. Signs and Symptoms

Signs and symptoms are communications from the body to tell us and others that we are not well. *Signs* of illness can be seen, heard, or measured by your doctor. Warts and rashes and hypertension are all signs of illness. The first two can be seen, the third can be measured with a blood pressure cuff.

A *symptom* is a person's subjective experience of his illness; it may be pain or palpitations or nausea or fatigue or any one of a dozen other manifestations. Each person experiences his symptoms in his own way so that if he tells his doctor that he is having palpitations, he must explain *exactly* what he means. Perhaps he is referring to an irregularity in his heart beat, or perhaps to a strong pounding or thumping sensation, or perhaps to a faintness or lightheadedness. Pain has so many manifestations that we speak of high and low thresholds of pain to describe its intensity, and *specific* versus *free-floating* pain, but we also speak of it as *throbbing* or *sharp* or *dull* or *nagging*, et cetera. For obvious reasons, vomiting is considered to be both a sign and a symptom; allergies and the wheezing of asthma also play this dual role.

All these signs and symptoms provide a trigger to set off the alarm that in turn urges the individual to seek help, so he sets off for his doctor's office, confident that he has the requisite ticket of entrance. Most people, in fact, believe that they cannot go to their doctor's without that admission ticket, and so they wait until they have a symptom before they make an apointment. Some, like Jerry, even find symptoms too nebulous and actually wait for a physical sign before they go for help.

But even after the symptom has been communicated from the sufferer to the doctor and the sign has been investigated and measured, there is still the problem of locating the cause. In Jerry's case, for example, the symptom was nausea but investigation revealed no physical cause. Hypnosis finally indicated that the cause was family friction, but interestingly enough, the cause was not communicated in medical terminology; it was announced in idiomatic English that left no doubt about the meaning: *"You make me sick!"*

More and more often, patients come into my office carrying baggage containing not only symptoms and signs but also verbal idiomatic messages that describe the cause of their troubles. They seem to be unable to interpret these messages themselves and appear to be looking for someone to do it for them. For example, Austin N. comes into my office with a back problem. He doesn't know how he got it, he didn't have an accident but there it is. I ask him to describe his pain symptom and he says, *"Doctor, I feel like I have the weight of the world on my shoulders!"* Why does Austin have a bad back? His subconscious mind obviously knows, even if his conscious mind is in the dark.

Think of all the idiomatic expressions that we use to refer to our backs and the load they have to carry:

It gets my back up
Get off my back
Back off
Someone has to shoulder this responsibility
I feel weighed down
She's a pain in the neck

Every language has its own set of symbolic body-messages. I am, of course, most familiar with idiomatic English used in this way but it applies to every language, and readers who use English as a second language will be able to think of idiomatic expressions in their first language which seem to fill the same bill.

The multiplicity of phrases which refer to the back parallels the frequency with which doctors see back problems in their offices; sometimes I think that every new day brings me another bent back! The best way to ivite the sufferer to unload is through hypnotherapy, and I often find it is worthwhile to begin by asking the

patient in a very straightforward way whether he really wants to get out from under his load — another idiom, of course. Many people find, to their own surprise, that they do *not* want to get out from underneath and that, in some ways, the load they are carrying contributes to their whole image of themselves or that it is appropriate to their situation.

Sometimes, I can use the actual words of the patient's complaint: *Who's on your back?* or *What gets your back up?* Since in hypnosis we have usually put to one side our fears about what people will think of us, explorations like this are normally quite acceptable and therefore profitable. The person who practices self-hypnosis and who realizes that he is expressing his problems in this way may explore this area himself.

The gastrointestinal system provides another wealth of body idioms:

I get all choked up
It makes me sick

You make me sick
I'll throw that back at him next time
I feel all churned up about it
I've had a bellyful of it
I have a hard time swallowing that
I'm sick and tired of it all
I've bitten off more than I can chew

Recognize any of them as part of your own vocabulary? If you do, it's time to think about their significance. It has been my experience that patients who arrive in my office with one of these complaints, generally have an appropriate symptom or sign to go with it: *pain, nausea, vomiting,* or *diarrhoea.* When there is no apparent physical cause, it generally means that they had a need to be rid of something. In the case of diarrhoea, sometimes the need is so great that the person almost turns himself inside out trying to do it. Indeed, protracted diarrhoea can cause a prolapse of the rectum. But the ultimate condition in the gut is ulcerative colitis in which the patient erodes himself away in an effort to rid himself of his trouble.

I recall a little girl about ten years old who was brought to me from upcountry suffering from almost continuous vomiting. I took the referring pediatrician's description of her signs and symptoms with a grain of salt until I found out that indeed, twenty or thirty times a day, she brought her gastric contents up into her throat and then swallowed them again. This affliction interfered with her life at home and school and in social activities to a very marked degree. In fact, she was shunned at school because she smelled so awful, and even her family was hard pressed to treat her normally. Her parents were now desperate, her family doctor was desperate, and even the pediatrician who had investigated this youngster in every possible way was desperate.

In hypnosis, the girl had no answer when I asked "*What are you sick of?*" But she had no difficulty agreeing that she was certainly sick of *something.* Toward the end of our second session, I suggested that it would be all right if she was not sick on two of the days between then and the next session. When she returned, her mother reported that she had only regurgitated a few times in very small quantities on the second and third days after her last visit. Very pleased with myself over this success, and sure that I was on the right track, I suggested that between then and the next visit, she would only have to be sick when she wanted to be. This suggestion met with success too, but of a different sort; she vomited more than seventy times a day every day after that visit. I was quite willing to continue this line of investigation until she found out why she needed to vomit all the time because I was completely certain now that I was on the right track, but it was too much for her poor parents and they did not bring her back.

Ulcerative colitis can also often be helped significantly with hypnosis. The exploration can follow the lines I have suggested to find out what the patient is so desperately trying to get rid of. If the patient is willing to use this process, I usually suggest that he allows his conscious mind to forget what it has learned in hypnosis in order to avoid unnecessary hurts. Where deep analysis into specific causes might take too long or might cause too much psychic damage, I find it sufficient to ask, "Do you think that it would be all right now to let this tattered part of yourself begin to heal? Have you done enough now?" If the answer is yes, the subconscious will do whatever it needs to do to begin the healing process.

Many patients come to my office with skin symptoms — rashes, blemishes and itching — which reflect a myriad of inner disturbances. I had an interesting case of a young woman who was referred to me because she kept picking and scratching at herself. She actually had scars from the excoriations, and her face had been worked over by her fingernails so often that it looked like a teenaged nightmare. In hypnosis, she readily identified the source of the irritation as soon as I asked the obvious question: *"What has got under your skin so intensely that you'll scar yourself trying to get it out?"* Her answer was immediate: *"My mother-in-law."*

This was the situation: She was a girl from a strongly Protestant northern European family who had married into a Jewish family from New York. She and her husband had established a good marriage in spite of their differences but the young woman's relations with her in-laws were very strained. Her mother-in-law made no secret of the fact that she considered her son to have taken for a wife a woman unworthy of the tradition of excellent wifely virtues found in his own culture. And although the husband advised his wife to ignore his mother, the woman's criticisms got under her skin. Fortunately, the husband and wife moved to Vancouver after a while, so the young woman's troubles were somewhat reduced as her mother-in-law was confined to telephone calls, letters, and occasional visits.

In this case, the young woman had come to me not with a story of domestic problems or even an idiomatic message to interpret, but with the symptom of itching. I took a chance by interpreting her symptom's message as an indication that the cause lay in her subconscious. When she came out of hypnosis she asked with some surprise, "Did I really say that?" When assured that she had, she was quite willing to accept it because the message had at last escaped from her subconscious.

We worked on her problem for several weeks exploring better ways of coping, and the itching and scratching decreased, then stopped entirely. Shortly after this, the young woman became pregnant, but when the good news was telephoned to the family in New York, the mother-in-law decided to pay a three month visit. For the first month the young woman coped quite well, then on a shopping excursion to a neighbouring city, she had a spontaneous abortion. This set the mother-in-law off on another attack on her wifely worthiness and brought on another round of scratching. However, the young woman came back for a hypnosis booster and this was conquered fairly quickly.

There are many other situations where the body's symptom is a symbol that can be interpreted in idiomatic English. When investigation had revealed no physical cause for one young fellow's vague aches and pains in his knees, I asked him in hypnosis why he was not allowing himself to stand on his own two feet. This produced a rush of information and examination of his relationship with his parents. Too frequently parents exhort their teenaged offspring to stand on their own two feet, then continue to treat them, as this young man's parents did, as if they were still children. To the young, this is both confusing and threatening, hence the retreat into symptoms.

Much of the anger that people feel is never expressed verbally but it finds its way into doctors' offices in signs and symptoms. Beware if you pride yourself on never getting angry or, if you have a little more insight, on never *allowing* yourself to get angry. And look out for the couples who say, *"We never fight!"* These are the people who eventually express their anger in body symptoms and signs.

Rheumatoid arthritis, for instance, is found in people who carry around a tremendous load of suppressed anger. They are usually gentle, soft-spoken, long-suffering people, who are unwilling to bend in any way — and, of course, after a few years literally *unable* to bend — and *silently, furiously angry.* In a study reported by Robert Ader (*PsychoNeuroImmunology*, Academic Press, New York, 1981, page 161) he characterized rheumatoid arthritics as persons who "... were aware of strong unexpressible angry feelings, reacted oversensitively to the slightest criticism or rejection, and tended to court others' favour, allowing themselves to be imposed upon." Solomon and Amkraut (PsychoNeuroEndo-Crinological Effects on the Immune Response", *Psycho-NeuroImmunology*, Academic Press, New York, 1981) find rheumatoid arthritics to be "... restricted in the expression of emotion (especially anger), conforming, self-sacrificing, tending to allow themselves to be imposed upon, sensitive to criticism ... stubborn, rigid, and controlling." All this bottled up anger is expressed in red-hot, angry joints, but those arthritics who are able to appreciate the significance of the relationship between their emotions and their arthritis are able to ameliorate their symptoms by learning how to get their anger out.

Teeth grinding is another symptom of unexpressed anger. A man came to me because the lady with whom he was living had begun to complain that he was grinding his teeth so much that it kept her awake at night. He claimed to be unaware of the problem and that was probably true on a conscious level. But in hypnosis, it turned out that his subconscious was perfectly aware of the problem and of the cause as well. The teeth grinding was the result of his frustration at not being able to say the angry things he wanted to say, but in hypnosis he said them *all* and his teeth grinding ceased.

Insomnia is frequently a symptom of an underlying fear of death or of letting down one's guard. Society exacerbates this by referring euphemistically to death as "eternal sleep" or "gone to rest". and how many children have been scared to go to sleep because a much loved family dog has been "put to sleep"? I find it worthwhile, therefore, to explore this idea when dealing with insomniacs in hypnosis.

One insomniac who was referred to me, however, persistently denied all problem areas until asked in hypnosis whether she was afraid of letting some secret escape while she was asleep. She used ideomotor responses to tell me that she did not want to answer the question. However, since she was the lady friend of the gentleman who ground his teeth, I already knew what she was afraid of revealing in her sleep. She had been to Las Vegas on a week-long junket with friends, had lost money that she could not afford, had borrowed from friends to settle her debts, then taken the money out of the joint account she shared with her gentleman friend to pay off her friends. Her gentleman friend already knew what she had done and was furious about it but wouldn't let on because he feared that she would simply pack up and leave and he would never get his money back. And so throughout my sessions with her, the lady continued to deny that she had any stresses, or at least any that would keep her awake at night, now that her gentleman friend had stopped grinding his teeth.

Venereal warts and idiopathic forms of vulvitis (an irritation of the vulva) are usually signs of guarding the gate against unwanted intrusion. When asked in hypnosis, *"Who are you keeping out?"* most women are able to give a specific answer even though they had no conscious understanding that that was what they were doing. For some, the problem is guilt about masturbating; by developing warts to keep *themselves* out, they are constantly at war with themselves.

Some depressions are symbols of body image disturbances, either as a result of surgery such as a mastectomy or for medical causes such as a serious heart attack. If it is reasonable to suggest that the depression was brought on by such a disruption, that is, that it is a reactive depression, I can sometimes get immediately to the source of the problem by asking: *"Does it feel as if a part of you has died?"* Then through his own description of how he feels, the patient will often lead the way toward resolving the problem, usually in the form of acceptance of the loss of the part.

Laryngitis is an obvious body message. A few years ago, when my husband and I were on our way home from a trip to England, I spent most of the flight home rehearsing the things I was going to say to him when we got home, decisions I had made about future plans. I'd had a bit of a scratchy throat when we left Heathrow but by the time we landed at Vancouver International, I couldn't even say hello to the customs man! I got my own message that time.

Sometimes power struggles between family members are verbalized as body ultimatums rather than just messages. *"You make me sick"* becomes a threat to get sick if the individual does not get his own way. Then he proceeds to do just that a few days or weeks or months later in order to fulfill his own prophecy and/or promise. And then how could anyone continue to take advantage of or be cruel to someone lying on death's doorstep?

The most blatant example of this I ever heard was told to me by a lady at a conference in Boston. When this lady became engaged, her mother announced, "If you marry that man, you will kill me!" Well, the girl married him and the mother died of cancer a year and a half later, making sure that her daughter understood *why* she was dying. Fortunately, the woman and her new husband went for family therapy sessions. It took some time but the wife now understands her mother's threat for the power play that it was.

We should all be aware that how we speak of ourselves often reflects our body response, but we should also be aware that speaking out about our feelings can prevent body *dis-ease*. For example, if I can tell you that you are a pain in the neck, I am unlikely to suffer that pain in the neck myself.

Not too long ago, I found myself seriously concerned about a personality conflict among my staff members. I valued each one of them, but their daily battles were getting me down. I walked out of the office after one particularly horrendous day saying to myself, *"I just cannot listen to any more of this!"*

That evening, I went to a jazz concert and my eardrum ruptured spontaneously. As far as I knew, there was no prior inflamation, although I was aware that, being under stress, I was vulnerable to viral infection. What had happened in effect was that in order to avoid listening to my staff, I had gone to the extreme of rupturing my eardrum. Listening to my patients would never have caused it to happen because listening to patients is an acceptable thing for me as a doctor to do; listening to my staff bickering was not acceptable. After that, I didn't have to listen to them because they all felt sorry for me and simmered down. Eventually, of course, I had to deal with the situation head-on because I couldn't afford any more eardrums!

2. *Getting Your Symptoms Under Control*

A responsible person who develops signs or symptoms goes to his doctor in case he needs antibiotics or surgery or something else to correct his physical problems. But while the doctor takes on his share of the problem, the patient can be determining what led up to the situation so that he can take steps to prevent a recurrence. At the same time, he can be dealing with the symptoms themselves in hypnosis.

We know that emotional factors have a direct influence on the way the nervous system responds, and that this response in turn prompts the immunological or body defence mechanism to function. This means that each individual can play a real part in relieving his own symptoms and in fighting disease, particularly auto-immune disease.

To do our part, we need to understand that although any one negative factor in our lives will be of little significance to our health, when a number of them gang up on us, that's when we knuckle under. It's a concrete example of that good old maxim about the straw that broke the camel's back. Each of us can carry around 5321 stresses and negative factors, but the 5322nd is one too many.

We need to understand that with increased stress, we become more vulnerable to disease processes, because as we use up energy to cope with the stresses we succumb more easily to the agent that causes the disease or to the one more factor that makes us knuckle under. Therefore, symptom control involves learning to cope with stress in a more comfortable way, decreasing vulnerability so that your body is working for you instead of against you, and promoting healing or resolution.

Consequently, the techniques I use are aimed at restoring the body image through visual or other forms of imagery. To a patient who is going into hypnosis, I might say, *"Become aware of how your body feels, of how you are experiencing this state of hypnosis. What is it like for you?"* Some people feel they are light or drifting, some feel as if they are heavy or as if they are sinking down into the couch. Some people feel as if they are a little distant or outside of themselves watching themselves. Then I suggest that there are other body experiences or "awarenesses" that we don't have words for, but are part of each person's hypnosis experience. I invite them to become aware of them, locate them, and identify them for themselves, not necessarily in words but as an experience.

As you learn more about how your body responds and functions, especially in these subtle ways, then you will have more control over these functions and responses. In this way, we can sometimes rewrite the script to help people through change. That is, we can change the image of the disease to promote healing.

I can illustrate this concept most easily by telling the story of a forty-year-old woman patient who had suffered an endocarditis, a very severe heart inflamation. Her life was never the same after that: she couldn't cope with her job, she didn't sleep well, she continued to feel distress in her chest even though the doctors told her that everything was healed. She had a terrible time coping with emotional problems although she had coped well before. And she began to drink excessively.

In hypnosis, it gradually came out that she had become convinced that part of her had died during her illness, and if part of herself was dead, how could she go on living, how could she function? We began exploring this idea, using imagery, and talked about how tissues heal, and how scars are not dead tissues but are very strong connecting bridges, *living* bridges, between the tissues that have not been affected on one side and the tissues that have not been affected on the other side. I fostered the idea that tissues that were healing or had been healed, far from being dead are *vigorously* alive, tougher than they had been before. Gradually, as she incorporated this idea into her image of herself, she began to cope much better. And the last time I spoke with her she had quit drinking and had opened her own business.

For the man or woman who has had mutilating surgery, the emotional problems can be very severe because their bodies *have* been literally dismembered. These people need a great deal of reassurance that, although the body configuration is different now, it does not follow that the person *within* the body has been intruded upon. They can heal their self-images even though their bodies must remain different. I find I can often bring the situation home to them by putting them on the other side of the fence. I ask, "If one of your children had the same operation, would you feel she was less of a person?" Naturally, the reply is, "Of course not!" Then I tell them, "You must allow other people the opportunity to love you and think of you as the person you were and still are."

Gradually, in hypnosis these patients gain a sense of themselves as *healed* rather than mutilated. Of course, it helps immeasurably if they have a very loving support person beside them who is very open about the fact that yes, she does look different now, and yes, I did have to get used to that new outer image, but nothing has changed between us.

For the woman who has breast surgery I always suggest that she read *Three Weeks in Spring* by Joan and Robert Parker, because this is the story of a relatively young woman who found a lump in her breast and went on to have a mastectomy. In the book, she and her husband talk about getting used to this, but the important part of the story is that they did it together. She was so nurtured by his steady love and openness that they were able to work it through positively. It has also helped the outlook of mastectomy patients enormously that many prominent woman who have had mastectomies have gone on to lead their usual active lives. And it has helped even more than their husbands have not left them!

Another technique for controlling symptoms is to get physiology working for you, interfering in what has become a negative cycle. As an illustration, I have a referral patient who had been on thyroid replacement for many years because her thyroid gland was not putting out enough hormone to positively influence the rest of her glandular system. She understood that it was important for her to take this replacement but she wanted to see if she could do more to help herself. I described to her the various areas where she could initiate positive interference in the negative cycle she was trapped in. She could perhaps interfere with the neurotransmitters that give information to the pituitary gland which sends out the hormones affecting all the other glands including the thyroid. The next place that she might want to consider exerting positive interference is in the thyroid gland itself, asking each cell of that gland to respond more vigorously perhaps or to send out more potent hormone. The third place that she could interfere positively is with the tissue response to the thyroid hormone, so that all the rest of the glands and tissues that rely on the thyroid's secretions would be encouraged to react more positively to the hormone even though they are getting a lesser amount. She could perhaps find other ways of interfering through her subconscious; it was only necessary for her to discover which one was most appropriate for her.

She decided that she would interfere with the thyroid gland itself, encouraging it to increase the amount of hormone it made. She coerced her own doctor into letting her go off thyroid with the promise that she would have her blood checked every three months. That was about two and a half years ago. She has not taken any thyroid replacement since then and her thyroid levels are normal. She has more energy, her self-confidence has zoomed, and she does her self-hypnosis every day to reinvigorate and reinforce her thyroid activity.

This patient's thyroid problem had begun with an inflamation that markedly decreased the thyroid's function, and it had probably not occurred to her doctor that the thyroid might be able to function again now that it had healed. The potential had obviously been there, it just needed the stimulus to get it going again. So by taking away the artificial thyroid and stimulating the gland with hypnosis, she was able to make it perform properly again.

Mrs. F. J., aged forty-four, has many, many health problems. She was diagnosed diabetic at age fourteen, and has extensive advanced diabetic complications. She had a transverse myelitis (inflamation of the spinal cord) at the age of thirty-nine. These two major afflictions combined to cause a spastic paralysis of her lower limbs, and loss of bladder control. She had severe family problems and marital difficulties. And when the stress of living got too much for her, she would go into insulin shock.

We worked together for two years. She needed ways to regain some control, and found one way through hypnosis. One of the most interesting results of this work was her changing blood sugar levels. In the past they had fluctuated widly, causing severe reactions at both ends of the scale. This is how the situation changed during those two years:

	APR '78 to JULY '78	AUG '78 to AUG '79	AUG '79 to FEB '80
Blood sugar range	from 47 mg% to 450 mg%	134 mg% (fasting) 374 mg% (2 hours after meals)	remains about the same
Reactions requiring glucagon	up to 3 @ day	up to 8 @ week	none since Oct. '79
Insulin dose daily	32 units NPH 5 units Toronto	21 units NPH (as required) Toronto	remains the same

Notes on Terms Used:

Normal level of blood sugar in fasting state is 90 to 110 mg per 100 ccs of blood. This is written as "100 mg%".

Glucacon is an insulin antagonist that is used if the blood sugar falls too low.

"NPH" is a long-acting insulin; "Toronto" is a short-acting insulin.

Hypertension is another symptom that can respond in a similar manner. When an individual who is taking a lot of medication for his high blood pressure tells me that he wants to do something about it, I suggest that he can positively influence his blood pressure in several ways. He can influence the force with which the heart pumps, that is, the force with which the blood enters the blood vessels. He can influence the response of the arteries once the blood gets to them, encouraging them to be elastic, instead of rigid and unresponsive. Or he can influence the response of the tissues which must be "profused" or flooded with the blood from the blood vessels.

Most people choose to work on the response of the arteries themselves, which is, I think, the easiest course of action. The image, therefore, which the individual will establish is one of arterial walls (which are composed of a very elastic type of muscle fiber) becoming even more flexible and elastic so that they will be able to accommodate comfortably the force of the blood pushed through them. This comfortable accommodation will in turn carry the blood more easily out to the tissues which the blood vessels are serving. And, of course, if the blood vessels are more elastic the pressure within them is also decreased.

Many, many people find they are able to decrease their blood pressure significantly in this way. Some of them still require medication but much less than before, while others are able to go off medication entirely and keep their blood pressure under control with hypnosis.

In a small survey in my own practice, I charted the progress of four hypertension patients. Over the page you will see the interesting results.

Patient	James P. Age 64	Jessie F. Age 43	Trudy R. Age 55	Freda M. Age 48
Medications at 1st Interview	Lasix Aldomet Captopril	HCT	HCT Inderal Aldactone	Moduret Apresoline
B.P. at 1st Interview	200/114	180/105	190/110	220/130
B.P. immediately after 1st session	180/106	160/90	155/80	210/120
B.P. before 2nd Session	210/120	160/100	160/90	220/120
B.P. after 6 weeks	180/105	160/96	150/80	200/110
B.P. after 3 months	176/104	155/95	145/80	160/86
Medication after 3 months	Lasix Captopril	HCT	HCT	Moduret Apresoline

Key to Medications:

Lasix: a diuretic
Aldomet: an antihypertensive
Captopril: a cardiovascular stabilizer
HCT - Hydrochlorthiazide: a diuretic

Inderal: a cardiovascular stabilizer
Aldactone: Aldomet plus a diuretic
Moduret: a diuretic
Apresoline: an antihypertensive

Notes on Reading Blood-pressure:

The top number (the systolic) is the pressure in the arteries as the heart is pumping. The bottom number (the diastolic) is the pressure in the arteries when the heart is *not* pumping (at rest). As these numbers — particularly the diastolic — rise, there is a greater risk of such things as strokes and heart attacks.

Three main factors are involved in the onset of an asthma attack and/or allergic reaction: *an infective factor, an emotional factor, and an irritating factor*. To combat the infective factor, you can obtain an appropriate antibiotic from your doctor. This leaves two areas in which the patient can interfere, and at first glance, it would appear to be easier to interfere with the irritating factor, that is, the dust or pollen to which the person is reacting. But irritants in asthma or allergies can be both external and internal, and when they are internal, they become part and parcel with the emotional factors which may be reinforcing the response. So in hypnosis, when I say to my patients, "Let your subconscious mind go searching for irritating factors," I know that they will be looking not only for irritants coming at them from the outside world — that is, smoke, pollens, et cetera — but also for those irritants which are tied up with their emotional response to the situation.

I instruct them to do whatever is necessary to neutralize and/or recognize these factors. Consequently, I know that they will do the commonsense things like searching out all the hidden sources of dust and smoke in their homes, and avoiding wild roses in summer, but I also know that they will use their hypnosis to clear the emotional jungles *within* so that they can really control their own symptoms.

Chapter Seven

Managing Pain with Hypnosis

Pain is the most common symptom. It is involved in almost every disease, injury or illness, and has more varied manifestations than any other symptom.

With a little luck, if a patient comes to me with a specific pain in a specific area, I can find out what is causing the pain and initiate a remedy in a straightforward manner. The difficult problems arise when the patient has *free-floating pain* where there is no anatomical distribution that fits in with any known enervation pattern, and where there is no symptom complex such as you would get with appendicitis where the pain begins around the umbilical area and then gradually migrates down to the right lower quadrant, accompanied by nausea and vomiting and possibly some diarrhoea. People who have free-floating pain pose a real problem because the doctor has to decide fairly quickly whether this is simply a pattern that he does not recognize or whether this is psychogenic pain that has no anatomical distribution because it has no anatomical origin. This pain may be a symptom of something else that is wrong in the patient's life. It may be caused by anger or fear or some other strong emotion that the individual does not know how to deal with. It does not make the pain any less real, nor does it make its "cure" any easier, but it does make it different as far as medical procedures are concerned, because pain which does not have an organic origin is strictly a symptom, that is, *it is a communication that help is needed.*

1. What is Pain?

There are three main aspects of pain which must be considered when we are planning for its management. The first is *muscle tension*. It is impossible for a person to be hurting and not have some muscle tension because the natural body response to a painful sensation is to *splint* the afflicted area to guard against further harm. Unfortunately, this is one of the several ways in which the body fights itself, because a tense muscle is more painful than a relaxed muscle. So while the body is trying to help, it actually compounds the pain. Muscle tension, however, is one component of pain that we have an excellent chance of conquering because we can learn techniques to relieve it with hypnosis.

The second major aspect of pain we must consider is *inflamation* which is the increased blood supply which brings white cells and phagocytes to the injured or irritated tissues. This inflamation aspect, although more difficult to deal with than muscle tension, can be minimized by sending out positive messages through the hypothalamus. For example, it has been found that burn patients who have been given hypnosis lessons within four hours of being injured and have been taught to give their bodies the message through their hypothalamus that they are cool and comfortable have shown a remarkable reduction in the inflamatory response.

The third aspect is *suffering* and this means the extent to which the pain intrudes on our lives, interfering with everything that we would otherwise be able to do. Suffering is partially derived from the physical limitations due to injury; for example, if you have broken a leg you cannot go dancing. Of if you are 62 and break an ankle, and are left with some post-traumatic arthritis that prevents you going hiking anymore, you are apt to suffer more pain because you are deprived of your usual pursuits. Even people who are on large does of pain-killers still frequently experience the suffering of pain because the drugs they are taking prevent them from carrying out their normal activities. And they still have the memory of pain and the anticipation of the pain that will return if they don't get more medication.

The use of *Brompton's Mixture* illustrates this point very clearly. Brompton's is a concoction of morphine and a number of other ingredients designed to relieve pain for terminally ill patients. It is given at round-the-clock intervals carefully adjusted so that the next dose is given *before* the last has worn off. The patient never has to anticipate the return of pain so that this suffering component is instantly relieved, and after a while even his remembrance of pain fades. Consequently, as long as he takes his Brompton's at regular intervals, he can gradually decrease his dose until he is on a minimum amount.

Another contribution to suffering is the *anger* that we feel either at ourselves or others that this injury or illness should have happened. We turn this anger into pain. The non-smoker who spends an evening sitting next to a smoker may develop a painful cough. This coughing, while certainly helping to clear out the mucus that has accumulated as a result of the irritation caused by the smoke, symbolizes at the same time the non-smoker's irritation with the smoker for causing the problem and with himself for not speaking out honestly when he knew that the smoke bothered him.

2. Can you give me something for this pain, doc?

Your doctor can deal with your pain in one of three ways. The first is *surgical*.

It is an established medical fact that whenever a stimulus occurs, it will follow a neurological pathway to the brain where, if it is interpreted as painful, it will trigger a message to the body to withdraw. For example, if you touch a hot stove, the stimulus that zips up to your brain will register there as "Burn!", and the message that will be triggered in reply will be "Take your hand off that stove!" But if you were a fire-walker of Fiji walking on a bed of red-hot coals, your brain would not interpret that stimulus as painful, so instead of triggering a message to withdraw, you would get a message that everything was okay. Keep walking.

Those stimuli which the brain interprets as painful travel on identifiable pathways; in fact, we know exactly what part of the central nervous system that they are routed on. Therefore, for intractable pain, it is sometimes practical to make a surgical intrusion into that pathway, literally cutting the pathway of pain. Of course, this is a desperate course of action, and only resorted to when all other means of pain management have failed.

The second method of dealing with pain is the most common. Your physician can prescribe *medication* in the form of analgesics, muscle-relaxants, and antibiotics. These will usually deaden or decrease the pain sufficiently to allow normal function of the individual. In other words, they decrease the suffering component.

The third is actually a whole group of methods that utilize *the person's own resources*. They include biofeedback, acupuncture and hypnosis. Biofeedback involves learning how to control the autonomic nervous system which includes such things as heartbeat, sweating, and circulation. It was originally assumed that the pain control mechanism in both acupuncture and hypnosis functioned by increasing the endorphins, the chemicals manufactured by the body to deal with pain. Therefore, it seemed logical to researchers to compare the endorphin levels in patients undergoing acupuncture and patients under hypnosis. As endorphins are very difficult to measure quantitatively, the researchers enlisted the aid of naloxone, a morphine antagonist, one of the substances used to offset the effects of morphine in overdose cases. Since endorphins are the body's natural morphine, they found naloxone also offset the effects of endorphins, so they gave naloxone to people who were controlling pain with acupuncture and to people who were controlling pain with hypnosis. They discovered that in acupuncture, giving naloxone reverses the pain control, that is, naloxone antagonizes the effect of acupuncture. The assumption is, therefore, that those little needles cause the body to manufacture and release endorphins. But the researchers discovered that naloxone did *not* antagonize hypnosis pain control, and therefore, it must be assumed that hypnosis does not cause the body to manufacture endorphins for pain control. There is some other mechanism at work here, and researchers are still probing the secrets of it.

Although most of our efforts must be concentrated on the management of pain, we must not overlooking pain's importance as a communicator or as a warning or monitor. Patients are often worried about this, and ask me, *"If I don't have any more pain, how am I going to know if I'm sick or if I'm getting worse?"* Usually I tell such a patient, *"Tell your subconscious directly, or reassure yourself that your subconscious mind* **knows** *when it is important for you to be aware of the pain for some message or information."* At other times I tell patients who are worrying that perhaps we should work on diminishing the pain just enough so that they can do their housework for an hour or so, or get themselves to an important appointment or accomplish some other necessary task, while still allowing them to keep as much pain as they need to let the signals get through.

Another problem in pain management is the fact that some people feel pain is appropriate in their particular situations. Certain diseases are well known to be extremely painful; therefore when a doctor tells his patient that he has one of these diseases, the patient expects to have pain.

Some well-meaning doctors will say to the patient, "Well, you've got arthritis (or some other disease) and that's going to be painful, so you're just going to have to learn to live with it." The patient is then in a double-bind because he has been told by this authority that he is going to have to live with pain and therefore he knows he should have pain. In addition, at a deep subconscious level he is interpreting the doctor's message as: If I have to learn to live with pain, he must mean that if I don't have any pain, I won't live. I'll die!

I know of a quadriplegic with virtually no sensation below the clavicle, who is absolutely obsessed with a feeling around the rectum which he describes as pain. He interprets this as a symptom that there must be a tremendous load of stool waiting there to be evacuated so he constantly badgers orderlies to give him enemas. This has become a real management problem for the staff, but I think that if that kind of "pain" was the only way that I could be reassured that my body was alive, I'd hang onto it too and assert it as often as I could.

Another aspect of this business of appropriate pain is the fact that some peple, at a very deep subconscious level, have the feeling that others might accuse them of only pretending to have arthritis or some other disease if they were to admit that they did not have the pain that is supposed to go with it. People might say to them: "What are you complaining about? Why are your joints swollen when there's nothing wrong with you?"

3. Getting Pain Under Control

All the pain management techniques that I discuss here overlap. As a matter of fact, you can probably think of them as all part of one technique, but I have separated them here for convenience. As a result, when it sounds as if I'm saying something about dissociation that I have already said about substitution, it is because the two overlap in those particular areas.

Successful pain management begins with the release of the muscle tension component of the pain. This aspect can be demonstrated most easily by clenching your fist. You will realize instantly that it is uncomfortable but that when you release it, it is comfortable again. Some kinds of pain have a large amount of this component while others have only a small amount, but all pain has some muscle tension, so there is always a place to begin work when you are using hypnosis to manage pain. (For relaxation exercises, see SELF-HYPNOSIS AND EVERYDAY LIVING).

The second technique for dealing with pain is dissociation, that is, by separating yourself from your pain in some way. People in severe trauma do this spontaneously. In the emergency room, I often hear people say, "I don't remember having any pain at the time. It was almost as if I was outside myself watching it happen." That is dissociation in its purist sense. And this is the aspect of pain management that most people readily understand because they have either had this experience or heard someone talk about it or read about it. Therefore, they are willing to accept the idea that if those things can happen spontaneously and naturally, there is nothing wrong with making them happen deliberately.

Children, who do not quibble over the appropriateness of a procedure, are very good at dissociation. When I am setting a broken arm in the emergency room, I can say, "Now you give me your arm so I can fix it, and you can just go off in your own imagination and do something else. Will that be okay with you?" And inevitably it is. They understand what I mean and they dissociate. When the cast is on and I tell them, "There, you can have your arm back now", they have felt very little if any discomfort.

When I go to the dentist, I give the dentist my teeth and toddle off to Fiji because I hate that needle in my mouth and it's much more comfortable for me to take a vacation. I have a patient with cancer who tells me that when things get really bad she leaves her pain-filled body on the bed while she does her housework or watches television for a while. My colleagues who work on the ski patrol tell me of people with broken legs or hips who spontaneously or with a little suggestion have given the broken member over into the doctor's care while they go on with their skiing.

One of the very useful things a woman can do in the early stages of labour is to take herself away from her body as soon as she feels each contraction beginning and let the uterus get on with its work. At this time, the cervix is slowly opening up or dilating, so the contractions are not yet designed to push the baby out. There is no point, therefore, in the woman trying to push; she will only be fighting herself. She can do the most good for herself and the baby by lettting each contraction trigger its own hypnotic response to help her dissociate and she can give herself the posthypnotic suggestion that this will continue to happen.

This works extremely well through the first stage of labour up to about eight centimeters of dilatation. During the last two centimeters of the cervix's dilatation — the transition stage — the uterus begins to try out a bit of pushing so for a while the woman has both kinds of contractions going on. This is the most uncomfortable stage of labour because her whole body seems to be involved. It's too early for her to push, but it's hard to separate herself from the process. At this time, I usually suggest to her husband that he put his thumb on her forehead as a physical focussing point to hold her attention. Then as soon as the character of the contractions changes, I suggest that rather than dissociating, the woman integrates with the movement, going right down into her uterus at the beginning of each contraction and pushing with it. This is very effective in pushing the baby out.

The third approach to pain management through hypnosis is substitution, but there is more than one kind of substitute available.

The first substitute is a different feeling such as numbness or tingling or warmth or some other sensation that is more comfortable or more acceptable. The example that is most frequently given is that of the person who sits in the dentist's chair, then makes his finger numb and puts that numb finger against his jaw to "freeze" it. This is also the principle behind the technique I use when I am sewing up a small laceration for a youngster. I suggest he watch a television show where it is snowing and cold. His hand (or whatever appendage has sustained the injury) will become "really, *really* cold, so cold that he can hardly feel it!" While he is engrossed in the television, I do my suturing which is comfortable for him because all he feels is cold. He does not feel the stimulus of the needle.

I do most of these small operations without anaesthetic, because local anaesthetic causes considerable discomfort for a child, and if there are only a couple of stitches to put in, I can get them in there and be finished in less time than it takes to give the anaesthetic and wait for it to take. Besides, kids are so good at substitution that there is seldom a need for anaesthetic.

The next way to substitute is to choose a different place to feel the sensation. If you have a very bad headache, you can move the pain down into one of your toenails and get on with your business. This is not altogether acceptable for those who don't want the pain under any circumstances, but this was solved by one lady I know who transfers the pain of headache down to her toenail, then in her imagination allows the toenail to grow and snips it off. This is a way of making use of substitution to lead into dissociation.

The next kind of substitution is to find a different time for the pain. This is one that people do quite spontaneously. The athlete who is injured in a competition pays no attention to his pain; frequently, he is not even aware that he is injured. Later, when he has the time, he will experience pain. The woman who is burned in a fire goes back to the building to rescue her child; she does not feel the pain of her own burns until later. It is common to hear people say, *"Oh, I don't have time for this headache right now. I'll just have to ignore it."* Or *"I won't let it bother me until I have finished doing this."* Or *"I don't have time to be sick right now."*

Or "*I couldn't afford to let it bother me right then.*" These people don't see anything incongruous in their statements because they look upon this form of substitution as a normal bodily function.

A fourth approach to pain management is by changing the image of the pain. The other three also change the image of pain in some measure but they do not cover all the ways in which the image can be changed.

To implement this approach, it is important for the patient to investigate how he forms images and what his image of pain is. Therefore, after I have given my patients an introduction to this type of management, I ask them to tell me about their image of pain, how they experience it, how they would describe it. Some might see it as a colour, or they might describe it by size, or mass or shape or density or composition or as a sound such as throbbing. Or they might say, "*It is just like a huge lead weight in my chest, doctor,*" or "*It was red hot!*" As soon as they understand what their image of pain is, then we begin to look for comfortable ways to change that image.

In New Orleans, Louisiana, Dabney Ewen, who is a consultant in general surgery, always uses hypnosis with his burn patients. He uses very simple imagery, suggesting to them that they imagine their bodies to be *cool and comfortable, cool and comfortable*. This suggestion is reinforced by the nurses and by the patients themselves many times a day, and Ewen repeats it every time he visits them. The result is that these burn victims have much less pain and they heal faster. Usually burn victims lose valuable body protein through the serum that oozes from their damaged tissues, but the burns of these patients to not ooze so they heal much faster.

The best example of a patient changing the image of his pain that I know of is the long-term patient who had severe pain in his left leg. When I asked the image of his pain, he described it as fiery red. He then decided he would find it more comfortable if he changed it to blue. When I pointed out to him that combining red and blue would give him purple, he corrected me, "It makes magenta," he said. Then he lay silent for some time in hypnosis before he announced, "I'm running out of blue paint." This was the first inkling I had been given of the mechanism he was using to change the colour of his pain, but I asked, "What are you going to do about that?" He said, "I guess I'd better go and buy some more." So in his imagination, he went to a paint shop, bought some more, and came back to continue his painting until his leg felt more comfortable.

It is significant, however, that his leg never did get really blue which would have indicated complete comfort to him; it became magenta which was *less uncomfortable* than red. I see this gentleman quite regularly and sometimes his leg is magenta but sometimes when he simply refuses to paint it, his leg is red. His explanation is, *"You know it's not that I can't do it. I can do it whenever I want to."* And he can, but sometimes he feels so angry he must have pain to focus on.

In managing pain with hypnosis, we are always aware of what we are doing. There are no tricks involved. We decide what mechanism we will employ and we decide how much of our pain to dissipate. Most people do not choose to be entirely rid of pain; they choose *analgesia* or the *diminution of pain* rather than anaesthesia, the termination of pain. But even in analgesia, although the stimulus still goes up the neurological tracks and back down again, the patient's perception of the pain has changed and his suffering has been diminished. There is less interference, therefore, in the process of living.

Hypnosis is often used — and should be used — as an adjunct to other kinds of pain control. There is no reason why the patient suffering from terminal cancer who is getting relief from Brompton's Mixture cannot use hypnosis to make himself even more comfortable. Nor should the patient who is recovering from an operation and being given analgesics every four hours not use his hypnosis to tide himself over between doses. Sometimes medication is absolutely the most appropriate thing to use, but you can always use a little hypnosis to enhance the medication.

Occasionally, a patient returns to tell me, *"I used some of your techniques and they made my pain worse!"* All I can say if *"Terrific! You're learning how to manage it. You're just learning it from the other direction first. Now let's go backwards and see what we can manage going the other way."* Even making the pain worse proves you can influence it. Anything you can do to change your image of pain or your experience of pain can alleviate the suffering that goes with the pain. In the beginning you may make only a small dent in it (or even a negative dent), but if you live with pain twenty-four hours a day, any change is something to hold onto. Even being relatively comfortable for ten minutes is a whole new ballgame.

4. Chronic Pain

Chronic pain is pain that is with the individual at least part of every day. Often it is there most of every day, and sometimes a patient will tell me that it is there waking or sleeping. This kind of pain is typical of terminal illness such as an advanced cancer and advanced multiple sclerosis. Advanced arthritis is also terribly painful all the time. Chronic pain involves the dread and anticipation of pain as well as the memory of pain, and this in turn causes dread and anticipation of the next pain. This cycle increases the suffering component of the pain immeasurably. Therefore, techniques and medication which will interrupt this cycle are very important, because once you break the cycle, you can use hypnosis to decrease your need for medication.

Chronic pain in many cases is linked to the suppression of emotions. In western society, in particular, the expression of anger is not tolerated so that children soon learn to disguise it or subdue it or withhold it. They learn even more quickly if they get punished for blasting off or striking another child or calling names. The energy that might have been released through an honest expression of anger has to find another mode of expression. They may do this by becoming very high pressure executives, highly organized but afraid to delegate power. They may do it through an obsessive-compulsive personality where everything has to be done with rigid control because if you have to control anger you will have to control everything else. They may do it through their bodies by putting all that energy into building up high blood pressure. They may do it through their digestive systems in colitis. They may do it through their joints with arthritis. They may do it through skin diseases. They may do it through some form of mental illness.

These are all ways that people deal with the energy that accumulates when they do not express their anger in an emotional outburst. Of all of them, arthritis is the most common. It would seem that rheumatoid arthritis, being one of the auto-immune diseases, is more likely to be the means of expressing anger than osteo-arthritis because the latter disease is degenerative and expresses a different kind of process — the aging process. It is the auto-immune diseases, where we literally wage war on ourselves, that are the very potent surrogates for the expression of anger. Consequently, it is when arthritics begin to understand some of this background that they can begin to learn some of the pain management techniques that will soften and neutralize that response.

Severe arthritics often make a great deal of secondary gain from their pain. This does not mean that there is anything imaginary about their swollen joints or their pain, but it does mean that their subconscious minds do choose to hold onto more of their pain than most other pain-sufferers. When you try to help them free themselves of pain, they will go so far and no farther. They will not go past a certain point of treatment even though going past that point might reduce their suffering so that they could resume activites they have had to abandon.

Now, while on the one hand it is a legitimate complaint that to go further might cause a great deal of pain or distress, the gain would be worth it if it would lead to an end to suffering. But in most cases, the arthritic will say very gently but emphatically, "I've had enough. It was very kind of you, dear, to take such good care of me, but I think I will stop now." If the doctor insists, the arthritic will just refuse with no overt anger but a dreadful amount of *covert* anger. Why do they stop? I believe that secondary gain plays a large role in this. In an arthritic's home everything revolves around his infirmity. If he got better, his role in the family would change. Maintaining the status quo is *not an intentional manipulation*, but rather the fulfillment of a subconscious need.

5. Acute Pain

Acute pain usually has to do with inflamation, a response of the tissues to some onslaught such as infection, injury, surgery, burns, or a flare-up of a chronic condition. The most profitable approach to acute pain management is to change the image of the pain, and once the image has changed, you can continue to use hypnosis to promote healing. By suggesting to yourself in hypnosis or by your therapist's suggestion, your subconscious mind will go looking for any irritating factors such as the infection or burn as well as other kinds of irritation such as emotional responses. When they are found and identified, they can be taken care of both consciously and subconsciously, and this will help the inflamation to decrease. As it subsides the swelling will go down and as the swelling goes down the pain will diminish and healing occur.

6. Headaches

The pain of headache requires a special section because headache is so universal. The two kinds that doctors have to deal with most frequently are the so-called tension headache and the migraine headache.

Tension headaches are not so-named just because the individual is emotionally tense; they are called that because of the tension of the muscles particularly at the back of the neck, across the forehead and into the temples. The best "double whammy" for the pain of tension headaches is to use hypnosis to release muscle tension and then go looking for emotional-psychological stress factors and deal with them both consciously and subconsciously.

True migraines are uncommon and only a small fraction of the people who believe they have them actually do have them. The symptom complex of migraine headaches has very definite characteristics. For example, they have an aura that tells when they are coming on. The patient may see flashing lights or shadows or halos. He may have hallucinations or he may feel as if a cold wind has blown through him. The individual with a true migraine is often physically ill, vomiting and unable to stand. He is also photophobic, that is unable to tolerate light.

Migraine headaches have two components: muscle tension and a vascular component, that is, the blood vessels that supply the brain dilate. True migraine headaches, therefore, respond to Ergotamine or one of the related drugs which cause constriction of the blood vessels.

The most useful thing you can do for a migraine with your hypnosis is relieve some of the muscle tension in the neck and divert some of the flow of blood from the head to some other part of the body such as the hands. This is, of course, a biofeedback technique. Most migraine sufferers do this by making the skin of their hands warmer. The warmth comes because of increased blood flow through the skin capillaries.

Chapter Eight

Controlling Anxiety with Hypnosis

The people who arrive in my office with anxiety problems are usually responding to that niggling little alarm which says that the whole problem has gone far enough. It is causing too much interference with their lives. Unfortunately, they are unable to get hold of some aspect of the problem where they can begin resolving it. Almost always these people require professional help to identify the origins of the problem, clarify those aspects of it that the subconscious mind has been hoarding and begin the task of coping.

1. Fears and Phobias

A phobia is an irrational fear of or panic reaction to some object or situation such as spiders, snakes, or heights. Before any treatment can begin, it is essential to establish exactly what it is that the patient is afraid of, because in spite of the fact that he may have come for help because of his fear of spiders, for example, that may not be exactly what he is afraid of. He may, in fact, be afraid of all crawling things but since it is spiders that he sees most often, he may be convinced that he has a phobia about spiders. Very often, this is a "masking fear" and is involved with a fear of the body orifices being invaded, or sometimes of the skin being crawled over.

A fear of snakes often masks a fear of sexual involvement; therefore, when a patient comes to me with a snake phobia, my inquiries have to be phrased very delicately. One young man who came to me for help about this kind of phobia told me that it was absolutely ruining his life. His only family was a brother who had established his family in a beautiful old farmhouse just outside the city. My patient loved to go there because he and his brother had a very close relationship and he adored his young nieces and nephews, but the grounds around the house seemed to be alive with snakes. He couldn't step outside the door without catching sight of a snake — actually just a plain old garter snake — slithering into the shrubbery. And now he had begun seeing them in the city too, in vacant lots and flower patches.

"What am I going to do?" he asked. In the course of our first talk it came out that he was a virgin and that he did not find himself interested in women at that time. *"I guess I'm just a late bloomer,"* he said and laughed. Feeling sure that we had not hit the heart of the problem, I confined my first and second sessions to teaching him the basics of hypnosis and a few relaxation techniques. At the third session, however, when I returned to the question of his sexuality, he revealed that he was drawn toward other men but feared committing himself to homosexuality as a lifestyle so he had avoided relationships with the men toward whom he was drawn. After that was out, although we did work on snake de-sensitizing exercises, most of his snake problems were resolved as he dealt with his sexuality.

Identifying the real phobia is a slow and delicate process because the patient's subconscious has usually buried this information very deep in order to protect it from casual investigation. I usually begin my questions by asking what the patient fears is going to happen. *"What are you really afraid of?"* The answers to this are usually quite nebulous because the patient is really not quite sure. *"Are you afraid that the spider will crawl inside you?"* I ask. Sometimes, I am rewarded with an immediate, *"Oh yes. That's it!"* but more often a great deal of sleuthing is required. And in many cases, it has to be ferreted out of the subconscious in hypnosis.

The most common method of dealing with phobias is by de-sensitizing. In hypnosis, the patient is exposed to imaginary situations which include the object of his phobia, then he is gradually encouraged to face the real object. For example, in hypnosis, a patient with a spider phobia is encouraged to open a book which contains a tiny picture — not more than two millimeters square — of a spider. Then he turns the page or closes the book. The next time he looks into the book, which may not be until the next session, the picture will be a little larger. *"Will it be all right,"* I ask, *"to look at a slightly larger picture? If it is all right, you can turn the page to see a slightly bigger spider."* If the next picture is too much, he can glance at it then turn the page back. Slowly as the patient is able to accept it, the pictures become life-sized.

When this hurdle is past, I ask him to imagine himself safely in his house looking out the window. He will see a real spider on the porch but the glass will prevent any contact. Little by little we remove the barriers until at last he can look on a real spider in the same room. He then takes these experiences from hypnosis into real life.

Another aspect of phobia control involves finding out if the fear was triggered by some specific incident which the patient may or may not recall. Sometimes the patient will pin the blame on some event which his conscious mind tells him was the root of his problem. But in hypnosis he may realize that his trouble pre-dated that event. Then I ask if he knows what the real event was, and then whether he is ready to find out what it was. Sometimes the answer is no, he is not ready and in this case I explain that in the forthcoming week his subconscious will have done whatever is necessary so we can investigate this on a conscious level. This gives the patient time to process the information.

Later in hypnosis I will take him back through the experience, assuring him that he is safe in hypnosis, and safe in my office with me. On some level he will be aware of these reassurances and therefore he will find it perfectly safe to re-experience the event in this neutral way. The result of this experience for most patients is an *abreaction* or *highly charged emotional response*. After several repetitions of this experience, I usually suggest that the patient re-experience the event again in hypnosis but this time he should see it the way that he wishes it had occurred.

We have all looked back and said, "If only I had known then what I know now I would have done things differently." Most of us know that this is a healthy recognition of the fact that we did the best that we could at the time with the information that we had. It is this concept that we are making use of when we go back in hypnosis to re-experience an event the way we wish it had been, so that we can allow those softer emotions and feelings that we now have to neutralize some of the harsh, older feelings. In some cases, I also take my phobia patients back on repeated hypnosis trips to a time before there was any problem, a time when they felt comfortable. This also has a strong neutralizing value.

Certain phobias such as flying can be effectively dealt with by embarking on a *progressive-retrogressive journey*. For example, in hypnosis, the patient who fears flying imagines himself at the end of a successful flight. He is sitting at his destination, happy and comfortable, visiting with friends or relaxing with a drink and looking back with pleasure on the flight. Then he imagines himself at the airport, having just landed, pleased that he had such a smooth flight. Then he goes back to three-quarters of the way through the flight watching an enjoyable movie. Then he looks back to halfway through the flight, eating his dinner and talking to the interesting lady in the adjoining seat. Then he looks back to one-quarter of the way through the flight when the stewardess came around to see that he was comfortable and to offer him a pillow or a magazine or a drink. Then he goes back to the very beginning of the flight and the take-off when he knew that since he had been doing his hypnosis to prepare for the flight, he was going to be okay. And finally, he goes back to a time before the flight when he was actually looking forward to putting some of his hypnosis techniques into practice.

These then are the basic techniques that we use to deal with phobias: *identifying, de-sensitizing,* and *neutralizing.* Most people need help in these areas from a qualified hypnotherapist, but after they have achieved the initial break-through, they can begin to use their self-hypnosis to keep working on it and to become even more comfortable. And perhaps, now that they know how, they might even iron out a few other little phobias while they're at it.

2. Reactive Anxiety

A panic reaction in response to a specific situation is known as a reactive anxiety. For example, Mary T. has written a terrific book and is to be interviewed on the local television station. She is panicky at the very thought of this because in similar situations in the past she has become totally inarticulate. This is a case of the subconscious blocking the conscious because panic is interfering. Mary must learn to subdue the panic in order to open the gate for the normal flow of information. Once she had become comfortable in hypnosis, I simply told her, "You know that you are a good writer and you have all the necessary information for this interview within your head and so you will find that when you are in front of the cameras the information that you need will begin to trickle through. And as soon as you identify the first piece of information, then you have something to build on and then a little more will come through. In this way, enough information will come to get you started and once you get started you will be fine." And that is exactly what happened when Mary sat down for the interview.

You will need a little help from a hypnotherapist to get you started resolving a reactive anxiety if you have had no experience before with hypnosis because you will need to identify all the aspects of it, but as far as subduing the panic reaction itself is concerned, once you learn how to do it, the rest of the job is just practice. After a while you will be so good that you can give the suggestion to your subconscious and it will do the job automatically. You won't have to stop and think about pushing the *Don't Panic button* anymore. Then finally you will get so good at it that the subconscious will take over before the panic hits. You may still feel a little "butterfly-ish" but it will be nothing that you can't cope with.

3. Free-Floating Anxiety

Many people live with free-floating anxiety every day of their lives. They wake up in the morning feeling panicky, they feel panicky all day, they go to bed feeling panicky, and they probably dream of panic. They tell me, *"I'm so nervous about something all the time"*, or *"I've always been nervous. Even as a child, I was nervous."* These people are in a desperate situation because they are always in a hyper state, they've always got the adrenalin surging through their bodies. Their hearts pound, their heads pound, their stomachs are in a knot, they can't eat, and they have diarrhoea all the time. They jump at the least sound and it puts them off for the next two hours. It's an exhausting business for them and they are fatigued all the time, but they are afraid to sleep because tomorrow may be worse. You can imagine what this does to their lives and to their relationships with other people.

This is far more difficult to deal with than the specific fears or phobias or anxiety reactions because it is so difficult to find a place to start on the problem. I usually start, therefore, with one symptom. *"What part of your anxiety bothers you most?"* I ask. *"Let's work on that. Let's soften it a bit."* Or if I think it would be more useful to start at the other end of the scale, I may ask the patient which symptom or which part of the reaction he thinks it would be easiest to get rid of. When we have begun to soften this reaction a little, it might be time to start searching through the past to find what started the anxiety. Usually it was not a single situation but a conglomeration of factors building up until one more factor came along and fell into place, triggering off the panic. Consequently, most patients do not identify any particular event but instead identify several difficult times in their lives.

A lot of free floating anxiety has to do with self-image and the fear of being unable to cope. Some patients are convinced that they are not good enough, that they are inadequate, that they are stupid. Often it involves a family situation where an efficient older brother or sister or parent or spouse takes pains to point out the patient's stupidity.

Because of the constant adrenalin surge, people suffering from free-floating anxiety have the potential to be enormously energetic but all their energy goes flying off in every direction. So the image that I suggest to them when we begin the task of harnessing their energy is that of radiating light beams.

"*Imagine,*" I tell my patient, "*that your energy is like light beams that you are throwing out in all directions. Let's work on gathering up some of those beams and harnessing them, putting them to use in a definite direction. Is there a project that you would like to start thinking about where you can start directing this energy?*" In most cases, there is something that the patient would like to finish, something that was abandoned when the anxiety took over. So in a hypnosis image, we gather up some of the energy, focus it and direct it. The patient still radiates the same amount of energy because we haven't done anything about that yet, but the process of gathering it up and focussing it and doing something useful with it is therapeutic in itself. The patient is accomplishing something practical

After this, it is time to go back to identify the elements of the anxiety to find out what he is afraid of. Many of my free-floating anxiety patients are afraid of losing control and this is exactly what they do. They are afraid that when they are out in public they will disgrace themselves by fainting or starting to scream or becoming hysterical or being unable to talk. Other patients fear lapsing into unconsciousness or fainting because they are afraid of dying. Since this is aggravated by the fact that they do not understand what happens when they faint, it is sometimes useful to explain that fainting is nature's way of giving the individual two or three minutes to gather himself together.

Because there is rarely a specific cause to go back to, I almost always take my patients back in hypnosis to a time before their problems began. I have no way of knowing when that time was, and for the most part my patients don't know when it was either, but the subconscious always knows and obliges by taking the patient back to that comfortable time. In the next phase of the treatment, the subconscious is encouraged to come toward the present, clearing the intrusive factors that it meets in that journey. And because it is clearing each factor as it meets it and not trying to do everything at once, this can be managed successfully. As a result in the course of the next few visits, I begin to hear comments like: "*You know, I don't know what's different but I feel better. I had four hours sleep last night! I haven't had four hours sleep in a row for three years!*" Or "*I was able to go out and do my own shopping and I feel really good about that!*" Very often we never discover the exact source of the anxiety, but that is immaterial if the patient has learned to cope better.

Before my patients leave me, I teach them techniques to bolster their self-confidence and strengthen their egos. They learn to make positive assertions about themselves such as: *I know I can do this, I can do this, I feel well, every day I am coping better, I am learning to use the resources within myself.* I remind them that they have within themselves a pool of resources that is always, always there. Sometimes the pathway to it gets tangled but you can clear that pathway with hypnosis. Imagine your hypnosis as a scythe that you can use to clear the path so you can get down to your pool of resources. Then spend a little time at that pool, gather up what you need to refresh and restore yourself. You can go to that pool whenever you want because it is always there. It is within you and comes from within you and no one can ever take it away from you. Sometimes we give away the things that come from within us, sometimes we even throw them away, but no one can ever take them away.

This is a very positive statement of the patient's own competence and ability to cope with his problems. On his own he uses his self-hypnosis to foster and encourage his belief in himself, so that in a few months' time no one would ever know that he had had a problem with anxiety.

4. *Agoraphobia*

Agoraphobia is a fear of open places. It is not your everyday run-of-the-mill phobia because, like free-floating anxiety, it intrudes into absolutely every corner of the person's life. People who suffer from it are afraid to go out of the confines of their secure place in case they find themselves in a situation that they cannot handle.

There is a lot of controversy about the cause of agoraphobia but the main theory is that it begins when people are forcing themselves, or are being forced, to do something that they really don't want to do, such as going out to take a job they don't like or going to a school that they don't want to attend. They become angry when forced to do it but at the same time they are aware that it is not appropriate to be angry about it because it is a perfectly normal thing to do. Subconsciously, therefore, they begin looking for ways to avoid it, and one way to do this is to be so afraid of going out that they dare not leave the house.

The outside world becomes a menace and the inside world where they are secure gives them a place to hide. Most of the agoraphobics that I have worked with are very comfortable in their own homes. In fact, on one occasion, I made a house call to do hypnosis with a lady who not only functioned perfectly well in her own home, but was a good homemaker and welcomed people coming to visit her. But she could not leave her home even to do her own shopping; while I was there, her mother arrived with her groceries! If you asked her what she was afraid of out there, she would not have been able to tell you. For agoraphobics, the fear is always undefined or at least there are no words to describe what they are afraid of.

5. *Claustrophobia*

Claustrophobia is the reverse side of this coin; it is a fear of enclosed spaces. Those afflicted by it run the whole gamut from people who simply prefer to take the stairs instead of the elevator to people who literally cannot go into any space smaller than a warehouse and always have to check for exits before they enter. Sometimes people who say they are afraid of flying are really afraid of small enclosed spaces. It is claustrophobia that attacks as soon as the airplane door closes and they are trapped.

Some experts associate claustrophobia with a fear of death or more particularly with fear of a coffin.

Most claustrophobics can find some way of avoiding situations which are confining or have no exits. For example, they can take the stairs instead of the elevator even if it is a long way up.

In hypnosis, claustrophobics can often be conditioned into entering *large* enclosed places by first making certain that they know where the exits are and by allowing them to sit near one. At first, they only remain in the room for five minutes at a time but gradually they increase the time and decrease the size of the room. On an imaginary elevator trip, they can imagine a nice window in the elevator looking out into a beautiful garden. In this way they can manage to take short trips.

Then I can suggest that instead of taking the elevator to the eighteenth floor, they should just take it up to the second floor, then walk two or three floors and then they might want to take the elevator again. Another hypnosis image that is useful is that of an imaginary friend who is in fact their own self. This friend can cope with anything so they can absolutely rely on him to help them cope with claustrophobic situations.

Chapter Nine

Controlling Life-Style Habits

Nobody changes a life-style habit until the reason for changing becomes more important than the reasons for continuing in the old pattern. Changes made for any other reason are only temporary. This is why if you go to a "weight loss clinic", you will lose weight but you will put it all back on again in a short time. The reasons for your old eating habits have not changed; they have only been overlaid with an immediate response to a situation. When that response has worn off, you will be stuck with your old eating habits again. So it is vital to find out what your reasons are for maintaining your present habits before you embark on changes.

Most of our reasons for staying fat or continuing to smoke or biting our nails stem from the rewards we get from doing them. They are not rewards that our conscious minds are aware of nor are they any longer particularly valid. They are also usually well-hidden because if they weren't and we could discover them easily and examine them closely, we would immediately quit the habits that were not good for us. It is because people are not aware of these rewards that they are not able to maintain the changes in their habits that they think they want to make.

The hidden rewards have some basic characteristics in common. Most of them, but especially those involving weight, began long ago, usually in childhood. They were almost always appropriate at the time they began. For instance, the child who survived the depression of the thirties becomes the man who still pinches every dollar till it squeaks even though he has a million more of them in the bank, because he is still living the way it was important to live when he was a child.

Hidden rewards are also usually involved in maintaining a role that sustains the ego. A fat lady cannot lose weight because her subconscious knows that she could no longer play the role of the jolly fat Mama and that is the only role she knows how to play. A young man cannot give up his cigarettes because of his swinger image.

Sometimes secondary gains play a part in maintaining inappropriate life-style habits. For the most part, these gains are just under the surface of awareness and would be easily seen if the individual wanted to see them. Fortunately, this is not a very common reason for developing a life-style habit.

In the next two chapters, we will investigate the use of hypnosis in the control of *weight problems, smoking, medication dependence, insomnia,* and a *number of nervous habits.*

1. *Pound Problems and Hypnosis*

People with too many pounds may be divided into two categories: *the overweights and the obese.*

The overweights are people who need to lose a little weight, anywhere between five and twenty pounds. Maybe even twenty-five pounds. To anyone looking at them, they do not appear particularly fat, but they know that their bodies are not in the right proportions. Their clothes don't fit quite right, their bellies swell out over their belts, and their shirtfronts gape between the buttons. They feel pudgy. They have too many pounds for comfort.

Overweights are often yo-yo dieters. They take off ten pounds on the current fashionable diet, but next year they put the ten pounds back again with an extra two pounds for interest. When bathing suit time comes around again they take it all off on a crash diet of grapefruit and yoghurt and by Christmas it's back in place with three more pounds to boot. And this goes on until they are carrying twenty pounds more than what is appropriate for them. They will never lick their problem with crash diets because they regard a diet as something to be suffered through, and when it's over they can go back to eating normally again. But as soon as they return to their normal eating habits, they put on weight again. *What's going wrong?* they ask.

Most of these people do not realize that their body metabolism has changed from the way it was when they were sixteen or twenty. What was normal eating for them at that age is overeating at their present ages. They are taking in more calories than they can possibly expend so those calories pile up in fat stores.

When I tell housewives that they must do more exercise to use up their extra calories, they wail at me, *"But I'm on the go all day!"* Of course they are, but it's not the kind of exercise that works off the pounds. They need to take time for themselves each day with a regular exercise regimen. Then they need to find out how much food they require to maintain the weight they feel is appropriate for them. After that, they must stick to just what they need.

Women have the added problem of changes in hormone balance at various stages of their lives: at puberty, during pregnancy and lactation, and during the menopause. Each of these times requires a change in calorie intake; there's no sense eating the same way at forty as you did at fourteen because your metabolism has changed gears in between.

Overweight pounds can be attacked head-on with hypnosis. You can program yourself very simply by giving yourself suggestions for eating less (no between meals snacks, no desserts on weekdays) and reminders about regular exercise. But if you are looking for further help with your unwanted pounds, read the following section on obesity. Any of the techniques and "gimmicks" suggested in that section will be of equal use with your smaller problem.

2. A Larger Issue

An obese person is usually characterized as one who needs to lose more than thirty pounds, but in fact most people in this category usually need to lose between fifty and one hundred pounds. People who do not have the problem of obesity are prone to say things like, *"All those fatties need is a little more willpower!"* THIS IS NOT TRUE. The problem of obesity does not concern willpower at all; it concerns self-image and identity, for once a person has developed a "fat" self-image, it is very hard to substitute a new thinner one. As a result, therapists who work with the obese are constantly frustrated because the rewards are so hard to achieve, they are so few and far between, and the involvement between patient and therapist is, of necessity, so complete that it is almost strangling for the therapist.

I work with my obesity patients in groups because I have found that the support which group members give to one another is better than anything that I can give alone. Each person in the group recognizes a kinship with the others that gives her courage to persevere. She knows that she is not alone with her problem. On occasion, an individual who is merely overweight has joined one of my Obesity Control Groups and the chemistry within the group has changed drastically. The obese people become very hostile to the overweight person. Said one obese lady, *"People like that have no idea, **absolutely no idea,** what it feels like to be fat!"* And maybe she is right.

3. The Hidden Rewards

It is important for the obese to understand why they have done this to themselves. What are the hidden rewards of obesity? Why are these people not taking off the weight that they think they want to take off? Why is weight a continuing problem?

Most of the rewards for obesity began in childhood although they may not have been reflected until later life, but all of them began for reasons that were appropriate at the time. They may have begun with a mother who demanded that her child clean up her plate or she wouldn't get any dessert, or a child who ate the cookies and candies that Granny pressed on her so Granny would not be hurt. Or the child brought up on a farm who ate enormous meals to get the energy he needed for his farm chores.

In every case, the response was appropriate at the time, that is, it met the expectations of the adults involved, but it became inappropriate as the years went by and conditions changed. Forty years later, the little girl who has become a beautician should not still be gobbling cookies and candy, and the farm-boy turned accounts executive should not still be cleaning his plate and asking for seconds. It is important for these people to recognize that the situation has changed. There is no need for them to perform as they did when they were children.

Sometimes, the reward for obesity is the need to maintain a role. A voluptouous lady meets and marries a man who declares, *"I like my women **big**!"* So she gets bigger and bigger and bigger. An overweight man with a good sense of humour soon becomes a jolly fat man and finds the ego rewards are worth the extra pounds.

In hypnosis, I ask each member of the group to look for the hidden rewards that set the pattern for her long ago. Then together we set about reversing the process. To begin with, the individual must recognize that the subconscious has been sending signals to the conscious mind that have become **outdated.** Although they were once perfectly appropriate, they are now inappropriate but the subconscious has never been informed of the change. It is time now in hypnosis to explain to the subconscious that the situation has changed and that its signals are no longer valid. Although the subconscious must be thanked for staying on the job in the protector's role, it is time to start building a new mechanism.

Short term goals in weight loss have far more advantages than long term goals. I do not mean to imply that there should not be some eventual long term goal, but just that it is self-defeating to set your sights on losing sixty or a hundred pounds at one crack. Just the thought of it is enough to make most people give up before they begin. It is far more useful, therefore, to begin thinking in terms of five pounds or two pounds or even one pound. This lessens the risk of failure, promotes an encouraging situation, and gives time for the individual to get used to a new self. Someone who has weighed two hundred and thirty pounds for twenty years can find it disturbing to only weigh two hundred and fifteen. I've had patients tell me that rooms felt bigger and furniture roomier when they lost their first excess pounds. But the side effect which they found most disturbing was the fact that they felt diminished in their new environment. They needed time to accommodate to their new selves.

4. *Image Problems*

Obese people have an image problem that interferes with every aspect of their lives. They feel sexually unattractive. They avoid new relationships of any kind. They are ashamed to go out and get a job.

Obese women often feel that they must stay in the house and do housework. They belive that no one would take them seriously if they tried to do anything innovative or interesting. They think it is fine for a fat person to be a good cook or a good mother or fulfil any of the nurturing roles, but they will not risk attempting a role that would take them into the world.

The luckier ones, however, have learned to cope with their image problem by finding ways to bolster their personalities and compensate for their size. They have discovered talents within themselves or developed personality traits that are desirable in society, and from these things they have increased their self-assurance in spite of their excess pounds.

In my obesity control classes, we tackle image problems head-on. I give each person a large blob of red plasticine to make an image of herself as she would like to be. Then I hand out small "blob-lets" of yellow plasticine, each blob-let representing two pounds of excess weight, so if the individual has forty pounds to lose, she will need twenty blob-lets. Each person applies the yellow plasticine to her own red image in the places where she believes she is packing the most weight, usually around the thighs and midriffs in women, the bellies in men.

The red plasticine image goes home with its modeller, and every time she loses two pounds and keeps it off for two weeks she removes one yellow blob-let. This is active, wide-awake hypnosis; the only difference between it and ordinary hpynosis is that the image created can be manipulated with the hands to reinforce the idea, not just brought into focus when the eyes are closed.

Many obese people have not looked in a full-length mirror for years; they are careful only to look in mirrors which show their image from the breast up. But to tackle obesity, they must first acknowledge what is there, because *you cannot change what you do not know about.*

In hypnosis, I invite my patients to imagine a private room that has walls, floor and ceiling entirely lined with mirrors. Because the room is completely private, it is safe for them to enter and really look at themselves. What they see there is what their subsconscious minds can bear to see. Maybe it is not the entire truth about their size, but it is more of the truth than they have acknowledged before.

I then invite them to look up in the corner of the mirror directly in front of them where they will find a magic mirror which will show them what they are going to look like when they finish this project. This is the image they will focus on for the future. From time to time in the course of these sessions, I will invite them to return to the mirror room to see the improvement they have made and check on the image in the magic mirror.

This is my one concession to long range goals.

5. *Eating for One*

I promote the use of gimmicks to improve eating habits, because I firmly believe that *there is nothing wrong with a good gimmick as long as you know it's a gimmick.* And whatever improvement you can make with the gimmick you choose to use can be reinforced with hypnosis to keep your motivation high.

I begin the search for a good gimmick by asking my patients to keep track of everything they eat for two weeks. They don't have to show their tally-sheets to me or to anyone else as this is only an exercise to help them to recognize their own eating patterns. It can also be a useful guide for selecting a slimming gimmick that is appropriate to their needs.

One of the most popular gimmicks for my group members is The Blacklist. The patient simply chooses one food she will never, never, never eat again. I encourage them *not* to choose a food they adore or one that they eat as a regular part of their diet. It would be unrealistic to put bread on the Blacklist because that would make it a daily temptation. Potatoes might go on the Blacklist, however, because rice or pasta could be substituted, but if the patient adores potatoes they would not remain blacklisted for long and the patient would suffer an unnecessary defeat. The food chosen may even be one that the patient is not fond of; it is only necessary that it should be one that will stay on the Blacklist. I recall one lady heading her Blacklist with oysters. *"I hate the things,"* she told me, but it was an ego boost for her to get something down on her Blacklist, and later she was able to put things on it that were real denials. And they stayed on her list, too.

Another gimmick is Packing the Basket. After dinner, the patient sets aside all the food she plans to eat the next day. This is her personal picnic basket. It doesn't matter how much food she sets aside, nor does it matter when she eats it—she can gobble it all for breakfast if she wants—but this all the food she is allowed the next day. Allied with this one is the device of going grocery shopping only on a full tummy.

Lent is not only a religious event but a good weight loss gimmick. You can deny yourself something you really like for Lent—say, sugar—and see the difference it makes. Reinforce your denial with hypnosis, then monitor your sugar intake carefully after Lent is over to maintain the weight loss.

Make bets with family or friends or even with yourself. Bet real money on your denials. No candy for three months or you have to pay your brother Albert fifty dollars. Make bets with a friend who is also losing weight. First one to eat a dessert owes the other a new tennis racket or a bathing suit.

6. The Beloved Saboteurs

For obese people working on weight loss, the *beloved saboteurs* are the people who have the greatest emotional meaning to them: *mothers, spouses, siblings, and children.* They can make life so difficult for a person on this kind of a project that it is almost impossible for him to continue.

They are the mamas who overwhelm the dieter with encouragement, so much encouragement, in fact, that the dieter is stuck with his project in the forefront of his consciousness every waking moment. *"Alfie, every day you get thinner and thinner!"* says mama, but Alfie knows he has not lost an ounce in two weeks, and mama's little reminder is a wound to his ego.

The beloved saboteurs are the spouses who say, *"You don't need to lose weight, honey. I like you just the way you are!"* They are the friends who say, *"Good Lord, are you on another diet? What happened to the last one?"*

I have a cartoon strip from "Cathy" pinned to my office wall. It shows Cathy's mother arriving with a big cake for the constantly dieting Cathy. The next squares show Cathy denying herself the cake, then the penultimate one shows her frantically gobbling it. In the final square she says, "My mother has done it to me again!" And it is true that her mother has performed the office of beloved saboteur, but Cathy is also guilty of shifting the responsibility to her mother.

Confronting the beloved saboteurs is very difficult. How do you tell your mother or your wife to quit undermining you? Or how do you explain the kind of support you really do need? Sometimes it helps to use the betting gimmick with such people and sometimes you can enlist their support with the Lent gimmick, but often the only solution is a direct confrontation with the saboteur and a clearing-the-air discussion. It isn't easy to do but for the sake of your health it is worth it.

7. Battle Plans

Once an obese person has initiated an improvement program, he has to develop battle plans both to sustain his weight loss and to deal with crises that he used to respond to by putting his hand into the cookie jar. What other avenues are open to him in a stressful situation? How does he prepare for people treating him and responding to him differently as a thin or thinner person? What does he say or do when someone greets him on the street with *"Good heavens, you've lost weight! Have you been sick?"* or an office mate says, *"Gosh, you're crabby. Why don't you get off that diet?"* How does he adapt to his new role in the family? If he's not Big Daddy anymore, what is he? There's a real identity crisis looming for such people.

These are difficult situations to deal with while maintaining weight loss. Battle plans are needed, so in hypnosis, we imagine each of these situations and learn how to cope with them. We line up the reinforcements in this way before the real battle begins. These sessions have the added value of allowing the patient to learn more about his self-image in a safe and secure place. If he chooses to "forget" these rehearsals when he comes out of hypnosis that is his choice, but like all events taking place in our subconscious minds, the processing goes on long afterwards.

8. Keeping your Strength Up

Obese people often complain that they can't stay on a diet because they have to eat to keep their strength up. Or sometimes they tell me that if they don't eat, they'll get sick. Occasionally, it's "*I have to eat a lot to keep up my stamina because I work a lot longer hours than most people.*" Women are sometimes convinced they must be physically big to deal with their jobs. A mother of eight believes her size is the thing that keep her tribe in line. A woman executive believes she must be large to maintain her control over the men in her organization. These people are using their obesity as a buffer against the slings and arrows of fortune, but all of these excuses are really only power strategies.

In hypnosis, the patient can examine his own strategy and understand how he uses food and eating and his size to gain power. Gradually, he can take more and more responsibility and rely less and less on dominating others with sheer bulk. He can find his strength in a new image.

9. Reinforcers

When the pounds are slipping off, how do you keep them off? Here are some reinforcers you can use all by yourself once you've made a start on your project.

1. *Give yourself a hypnosis break.* Take two or three minutes to get a hypnosis refresher when you find yourself in a difficult situation. So you find you have parked the car right outside a bakery? Take two minutes for hypnosis and maybe you won't have to buy the cinnamon buns in the window.

2. *Use a posthypnotic suggestion.* When you are in hypnosis, prepare yourself for future temptations; then you'll be protected when the cakes are passed around after the Garden Club meeting.

3. *Give yourself a posthypnotic charm,* just a simple word that you can say when temptation comes along. It will help to remind you of your new resolve.

4. *Be aware of how you speak of yourself.* Fat people generally speak of themselves in a negative or derogatory manner. They say things like, "*Oh, well, I guess I'm just no good for anything else,*

ha, ha, ha!'' When you listen carefully to what you say about yourself, you will realize that you are reinforcing an image that you are working hard to lose.

Remember the word "try" is negative. Don't tell people that you are "trying" to lose weight, because they will know—just as your subconscious knows—that you don't intend to succeed.

5. *Use your hypnosis to get your metabolism working for you.* Fat people are often accused of being lazy, but generally speaking, they are not lazy but sluggish. Their metabolism operates at a slower rate than a person with a normal weight. Metabolic rate, that is, the rate at which we burn up food, is regulated by the thyroid gland, which means that a fat person with a "slow" metabolism is often suffering from an inefficient thyroid. This is not always the case, of course, but if you have a combination of general sluggishness, fatigue, dry skin, and a weight gain, it is definitely worth a visit to your doctor to have your thyroid checked.

To conteract the effects of a poorly functioning thyroid, you can use hypnosis to give positive suggestions to your thyroid gland to increase the rate at which you burn up energy. Once this process is begun, other changes occur as part of a chain reaction. The bowels become more active, the individual has more energy and looks for ways to expend that energy in physical exercise. And that same physical exercise gets the thyroid working even better.

In the past, patients were sometimes given thyroid replacement to help them lose weight. This speeded up the metabolism and did cause weight loss but it interfered with the thyroid's natural functioning, often depressing it so that when the replacement was discontinued, the thyroid could not resume its normal operation. With hypnosis, powerful suggestions are substituted for replacement, and the thyroid is encouraged to be more efficient in its function without any artificial stimulus.

10. It's a Big Job

There are only eight sessions in my obesity control clinics because this is the amount of time it takes to learn **how** to lose weight with hypnosis. But it's such a big job, that I continue to hold monthly drop-in sessions after that for as long as it is necessary.

For about two-thirds of the people who come for the obesity group sessions, the task is just too enormous for them to continue on alone. There are all the beloved saboteurs out there waiting to pounce, all the bakeries to walk past without weakening, all the daily crises to surmount. Ideally they require someone with them at all times to bolster them and keep their egos intact. Some find salvation in the services of an on-going clinic like the Metabolic Energy Conservation Assessment (MECA) at Lions Gate Hospital in North Vancouver run by the internists under Dr. John Hunt. There they find help in getting their bodies functioning more efficiently. (You can check in your city for a similar organization.) The remainder just drop out of the project and return to their old ways. The thought of taking off all those pounds is too overwhelming for one person alone.

However, it is a pleasure to report that many people on the obesity weight-loss program persist for years. Using realistic short term goals, they lose ten or twenty pounds, maintain that loss, and find it very satisfying. Perhaps their bodies need to shed another sixty pounds but it is far better to aim for ten and succeed than aim for sixty and fail to lose any. When these people have lived with their ten-pounds-lighter image for a time and feel comfortable with it, perhaps then they will be ready to set the next goal for themselves. In the meantime, ten pounds is still a victory!

11. Too Few Pounds

Anorexia and Bulimia are the other side of the Pound Problem. The true anorexic has literally lost her appetite; one of my anorexic patients, in fact, actually regarded a one-inch cube of cheese as a feast. The bulimic individual, on the other hand, goes on fantastic food binges and then gets rid of the food with huge doses of laxative or by making herself vomit.

Anorexia almost always occurs in young women, usually in the fifteen-to-nineteen age bracket, who have begun dieting because they were genuinely plump. They get locked into dieting, however, and in a short time become anorexic. There are documented cases of anorexia beginning in older women and even cases of young men suffering from anorexia but these are very rare. Bulimia generally begins around the same age as anorexia and is quite often the precursor of anorexia. Both seem to afflict individuals with severe self-image problems. These young woman may appear wraith-like to everyone who sees them, and they may be suffering from severe metabolic distress from lack of food, but when they look at themselves in a mirror, they see a fat person staring back at them.

Donna, a young woman who is recovering from anorexia, told me of her experiences in a clinic she had gone to for anorexics. Each person was required to lie down on a large sheet of paper while an assistant used a crayon to draw around her body shape. When Donna looked at the outline that had been drawn around her own body, she refused to believe it was her own form. *"It was someone far thinner than me"*, she said, yet she knew she had lain on that spot to have her outline traced.

There are many theories about the causes of anorexia and bulimia, but few proven facts. One theory says that they are the manifestation of a power struggle between the young woman and her parents. Those who espouse this theory point out that anorexic girls are most often intelligent, they do well in school, lead active social lives, are very obedient, and seldom rebellious. But by becoming anorexic they inflict the most disturbing rebellion of all on their parents. The parents try to overcome this rebellion by saying, *"But, dear, you must eat just a little!"* And that's exactly what the anorexic does. She eats *just a little*. This is a response to the implied hypnotic suggestion that she should restrict her intake of food. In this way, the parents, with varying degrees of insight, sabotage their daughter's return to normalcy.

Another theory is that these girls feel deep inside themselves that they are worthless and really don't deserve to live, perhaps because of some misinterpretation of events in childhood. They may think they are to blame for their parents' divorce or for a sibling's death. As a result, they are convinced they really should die and therefore they must not feed themselves.

Yet another theory is that the anorexic girl is afraid to grow up, afraid of the mature body of an adult woman and all that that implies, so she does everything she can to keep her body immature. Most anorexic women do not menstruate, so this reinforces the concept.

Whether any of these theories is right is immaterial to the therapy required because this is not just a case of using a little hypnotherapy to get the patient eating again. There are severe body image problems here that must be dealt with first. The anorexic patient must be given an opportunity to investigate her feelings about herself, her identity and her place in the world, and her image of herself. She will require a lot of ego-strengthening

and encouragement to take back control of her own life. Naturally, this cannot be conquered with hypnosis alone; psychotherapy
is needed to get to the heart of the problem.

In my work with anorexics, I find hypnosis most useful for ego-
strengthening and to help them regain a sense of self. More than
this is generally unprofitable as anorexics, though superficially
very compliant, will resist any attempt to induce them to eat when
they are not ready to. They will enter hypnosis quite cheerfully,
but they will tune out whenever the suggestions made to them are
unacceptable.

As part of the anorexic's therapy, I also take time to talk to the
parents about sabotage. *"Don't coax your daughter to eat just a
little,"* I tell them. *"Go into hiding for six months if you have to,
but let her find her own way!"*

Chapter Ten

More Habits and Hypnosis

1. That Last Cigarette

Most of the people who come to my smokers' clinics are already prepared to quit smoking. They are past the first hurdle. Consequently, I begin their hypnosis sessions by stressing the fact that by making the BIG DECISION, they are already in control of the situation. They are the victors. I am only there to teach them how to use hypnosis to complete the job.

We don't know exactly how long each person's subconscious is going to take to process its new information about smoking, but in due time the subconscious will deal with it and the individual will be ready to make changes in his smoking habits. Occasionally, after the first session of the smokers' clinic, a member of the group will quit smoking (thereby antagonizing everyone else in the group!). Occasionally, there will be a person in the group who goes through the entire course and makes no apparent changes whatsoever in his life-style. But most people begin making changes in their smoking habits *during* the course and continue making changes after it is over.

What is reassuring to those who seem to be immmune to change during the clinic is the knowledge that their subconscious minds now have all the necessary information on tap and can process it when they are ready. And when that happens, the necessary changes will occur. This is a positive thing to look forward to so there is no reason to feel frustrated. In fact, people often come back to tell me six months after the clinic is over that they have finally quit. *"I did it!"* they say. *"It finally took on me!"*

For smokers, the intellectual knowledge of the harm done to their bodies by smoking is of absolutely no significance. It is not important enough that they might get lung cancer. Or that they might get Beurgher's Disease in which the blood vessels go into spasm to the extent that the legs get gangrenous and have to be amputated. I have, in fact, seen a patient light up two days after his leg was amputated.

When smokers say, "I know I should quit smoking, but. . . .", there is a dissociation from what their intellect understands. So there is no use trying to rationalize the process of quitting with them because you only get into the morass of condemnation and blame.

My one concession to this aspect of smoking is an abreaction or negative reaction session I include in my smokers' clinics. I suggest to the members of the group while they are in hypnosis that they are lighting up a cigarette, then following the smoke with their inner eyes down through their respiratory tracts.

"Those little hairs lining the tract are called cilia. Watch how the noxious substances assault them, eroding them away. The cells are scraped and irritated as if they've been scrubbed with sandpaper And over there, those are mucous cells, working overtime to pro

duce extra mucus to soothe the damaged area. But the mucus settles into pools, partly because the cilia can't waft these irritating particles back up the respiratory tract fast enough and partly because there aren't enough cilia left to do the job. Those pools of mucus are real trouble because mucus is an ideal medium for bacterial growth. This leads to bronchitis and similar infections. And this is why smokers are constantly coughing.

"So now you are finished your cigarette and you stub it out. Your cells think 'Whew! Thank goodness that's over!' and they do what they can to start repairing the damage. But that's when you light up your next cigarette and it starts all over again."

Perhaps this session has an effect on one out of a hundred so I continue to include it for the benefit of that one person, but it is far more useful to stress the positive aspects of quitting.

2. Hidden Rewards

Most people begin smoking because of peer pressure, and when you are fourteen years of age and short on confidence, that's a good reason to smoke. But it's not much of a reason for still smoking when you're forty. Therefore, in hypnosis I ask my group members to examine the rewards they got from smoking when they first began lighting up to see if they are still valid today. If they are not, it is time to make a change.

We talk then of the future rewards of not smoking, and I ask them to write down what they will enjoy most about being a non-smoker. They list things like:

Saving money
Smelling better
Pride in myself
Food will taste better
Lungs no longer cancer-prone
No smoker's cough
Won't have to listen to my wife nag me about my smoking habits.

I encourage them to invent gimmicks to reduce their smoking habit. It helps, for instance, to put your cigarettes in a different pocket or a different place so that reaching for a cigarette is no longer an automatic action. If you don't buy cigarettes, you can't smoke them. Of course, you can always borrow, but your friends can soon make you feel pretty low when you do that. You can put certain rooms in your house or apartment out of bounds for smoking. You can deny yourself a cigarrette before ten in the morning, or noon, or maybe even three in the afternoon as your resolve gets stronger.

Most of our sessions, however, are devoted to postive ego-strengthening reinforcement through hypnosis, because people who have chosen to kick the smoking habit need all the bolstering they can get.

3. Pills, Pills, Pills

The lady had just read an article on the long-term effects of the tranquilizers she had been taking for the last twelve years. The article even named the specific brand she used, and she was very frightened.

"Nobody told me that they could do that to you," she said, *"or I'd never have taken them for a single day! But I tried not taking them last week and I nearly went hairy! What am I going to do, doctor?"*

Her story was very typical of the patients who come for help with medication dependence. Most often they have read an article or seen a television special on the subject and developed a sudden and disturbing new awareness. Others come to me as referrals. They have, perhaps, changed doctors and the new doctor in taking a history has discovered that their former doctor had prescribed Valium or some other habit-forming drug on which they then became hooked.

People begin taking medication—Valium, migraine tablets, sleeping pills, uppers, downers, sidewinders—because they are in pain from disease or injury, or they are in an extremely stressful situation, or they have just had surgery, all of which are perfectly valid reasons for taking medication. But some people go on taking medication long after the reason for it has gone.

In hypnosis, you can examine your reasons for taking pills, and by understanding that you had a valid reason to begin with, you can be reassured that you have nothing to apologize for. You don't have to carry the burden of blame. Probably no one ever explained to you that there are better ways of coping with stress, or that now that the worst of your pain is over, there are other things you can do to keep comfortable. Therefore, you became a victim of circumstances you did not understand and found yourself saddled with a physiological and psychological dependence — a bad combination.

Once you understand that there is a way to take responsibility, you are on the road to breaking your medication dependence. With people who are seeking to get off pills, I concentrate first on the hidden rewards of being on medication. In hypnosis, some patients discover that they continued to take pills because they could feel good without any effort; for others, it is the ego-boost of being thought of as someone who needs to be taken care of. Of course, these are not consciously sought out rewards; they are products of the subconscious.

We talk next about the eventual positive outcome because this is a powerful motivator. Why will changing be beneficial? THE FUTURE is the time when they will be completely off medication, when they will have regained absolute control over their own lives. They will be able to find resources within themselves to deal with their problems without medication. And the more often they can rely on their own resources, the more confident they will become, and in this way they will develop their own feed-back self-confidence cycle.

I explain to my patients that there are things that they can do to improve their own chemical balance so the body can cope more efficiently with its own stresses and pains. This is not done with hypnosis; it is done by becoming more active, by taking up jogging, or swimming or regular exercise classes. I talk to them about endorphins and about feeling good about themselves just as I do to people who are learning pain control.

It is time then to take back control of their lives, so that they become the victors instead of the victims. This is a weaning process, with hypnosis as an integral part of the treatment. I invite each patient to let his subconscious mind find out whether it will be all right to cut down on medication by one-half. The reply usually comes in ideomotor responses. If he signals "yes", then for the next week he will take only one-half of his accustomed dosage. If the answer is "no", we agree that the subconscious mind still has some processing to do before this can be acceptable. We must, therefore, go more slowly. Perhaps a third of the dose reduced, perhaps an eighth. Finally, we will achieve a figure which is acceptable to the subconscious mind. And this is great because we have established a place to begin working on the problem; even a tiny reduction is still a reduction. Little by little we can whittle the dosage down still further as the subconscious finds it acceptable.

For most of my patients the "Half and Half Again" formula is the best one. In this case, I encourage the patient to cut his dosage in half right now. Two weeks later we cut it in half again, so that he is only taking a half of the first half of the original dosage. In two weeks, we cut that half in half again, so that in this way, the patient can hang onto that last little bit until he is ready to give it up altogether.

The patient can keep his end goal in mind by experiencing in hypnosis what it will feel like to be completely free of medication. It's just a case of letting his subconscious carry him forward to that time to feel the satisfaction of having everything under control. He can even have a look at the calendar when he is under hypnosis and see when that lovely day is going to be; his conscious mind will forget that date so it won't become a burden to him, but he can keep his subconscious happy with the date tucked way down out of sight.

4. Sleep Problems

Many patients only come to me to get started on kicking the habit, to learn hypnosis and a few tricks to help them with the project. During my final meeting with one of these patients, I ask him when he is under hypnosis to set up a timetable to complete his project. If he has cut down his medication by twenty-five per cent, how long will it be until he cuts down the next twenty-five per cent? A month? Good. Eight weeks? Good. It is a goal to look forward to. But perhaps he cannot name a time; his subconscious is not yet ready to deal with the next level of the problem. Fine. I can assure him that his subconscious will give him a nudge when the right time has come.

Insomnia almost always dates back to a specific time or a specific incident when the subconscious learned that it made good sense to stay awake.

One of my patients is a lady who, after years and years of trying, had her first child when she was thirty-seven. It was a beautiful little boy who seemed perfect in every way, but at three and a half months he became a victim of crib-death. After my patient and her husband recovered from the shock of their loss, she began trying to get pregnant again. It took five years, but at last she did it. She was terribly ill throughout the pregnancy but she gave birth in due time to another beautiful boy who is now nine months old.

My patient and her husband are ecstatically happy, but she cannot sleep. She sleeps for half an hour, then lies awake for an hour or two, sleeps another half hour and so on. The essence of her problem is, of course, her fear that the child will die if she takes her eyes off him for a minute. It does no good to explain that he is past the dangerous age for crib-death. Her conscious mind already knows that; it is her subconscious mind that is still on guard.

Certainly, insomnia does not always originate in such a heartbreaking event, but every insomniac's troubles began with a problem that kept him awake. It might be a fear of death that developed after a child or spouse died in his sleep. Occasionally, it is a remnant of fear from a time of physical peril. Sometimes it is the fear that the patient might divulge some secret asleep; an illicit affair, a financial problem, even a crime. It need not be a current event and it might even be something apparently trivial, but the subconscious considers it must be protected at all costs. And the cost is sleep.

In hypnosis, we can pinpoint the incident or incidents that started the problem and find out whether the patient is ready to finish with them or wipe them out.

The solution is to take the insomniac back in hypnosis to a time before the problem began, back when his sleep patterns were comfortable and appropriate. Here he can experience the pleasure of real rest. The next step is to bring him slowly forward in time so that as his subconscious meets the factors which have contributed to his insomnia, it will neutralize them. How long this journey will take depends on the individual's needs and the difficulty of dealing with factors that caused the problem, but the subconscious will work through to the present once it has been put on the track.

The patient will soon realize that this process is going on because *little* changes will occur. He may begin falling asleep a little more easily, and occasionally get a full night's sleep. Or he may find that when he wakes in the middle of the night, he can fall asleep again after a while. This is the subconscious at work.

There are three basic ways to use self-hypnosis if you have difficulty sleeping:

1. You can use hypnosis to relax your body so that you drift naturally into sleep.

2. You can use hypnosis as a safe place to wait for sleep. The time can be used to plan the next day's activities or think about some pleasant event in your life. Since hypnosis-time is distorted, there will be no anxiety about the night passing while you are lying wakeful because your subconscious has received the positive suggestion that sleep will come when it is appropriate.

3. You can use a gimmick like the Blackboard Technique to induce sleep. In hypnosis, you will imagine yourself facing a nice clean blackboard and you will see your own hand take up the chalk and carefully write a large numeral "1" in the centre of the blackboard. You will admire it, notice its straight back, its perfect angle, the curlicues with which you have decorated it. You erase it, then up in the corner of the blackboard, you print the word "sleep" and erase it. You make the numeral "2" very carefully, erase it and print the word "sleep" and erase it. You make the number "3". How shall it look? Straight Bar on top or curved top? Roman numeral or arabic? Admire it when it is finished and then erase it. Print the word "sleep" paying particular attention to the vowels. Erase it. Numeral "4", "sleep", "5", "sleep".

Most people fall asleep before they reach "10", almost everybody before "15".

At the opposite end of the scale are the people who sleep all the time. I am not talking about narcoleptics because theirs is a neurological problem; I am talking about people who sleep to avoid dealing with the present or to avoid making changes or getting started on changes. They are not consciously aware that they are avoiding. They are only aware that they just can't seem to get enough sleep. There are no generalizations that can be made about patients in this category, except to say that no real progress can be made until the reason for sleeping so much can be dredged up from the subconscious.

One of my patients, for example, has given up driving because he always falls asleep when he drives, and he won't get in the car with his wife because he does not trust her driving. Or so he says. He also falls asleep whenever he has to write letters although he does not fall asleep at his job which involves working with pages and pages of figures every day.

In hypnosis over a long period of time, we learned that his compulsion to sleep stems from his relationship with his daughter. The only way he can get from where he lives to where she lives is by car; no other form of transportation operates between those two points. The only other way he can communicate with her is by letter because she has no telephone. But his disapproval of her lifestyle is so overwhelming and so heartbreaking for him that he avoids the problem with sleep.

5. Nervous Habits

Like all the other habits we have discussed here, nervous habits almost always begin when the patient is still a child. Eye-lash picking, for instance, often begins when the child has some mild irritation or inflamation of the eyelids and begins absent-mindedly picking at his eyelashes. Nail-biting begins with hangnails on busy childhood fingers. Tics, hair-picking and stuttering all have similar beginnings. In most cases, the habit is continued only when the individual is at leisure; as long as there is something useful to keep the hands occupied there is no problem.

Children outgrow some of these habits because their image of themselves changes. The nailbiter reaches her early teens and sees herself as a pretty girl with nice hands. The stutterer finds he is successful at sports or mathematics so that at long last people will wait to hear what he has to say. These "cures" are the result of spontaneous self-hypnosis, a straightforward message from the conscious self to the subconscious that the habit is no longer necessary.

But many individuals do not outgrow these habits, and in some cases the habit gets worse as the individual gets older. I begin work with these people by taking them back in hypnosis to a time before the habit began so that they can experience how comfortable that time was. Then I suggest that they can continue in that comfort now because they can manage very, very well without their habit. Its usefulness is over. They can now take back control.

Sometimes, when my patient is a child, I invite him to slip inside the person he is going to be when he grows up to find out what advice that grown-up self has to give him about his problem. Or I suggest, *"Let's pretend you are already grown-up and you are talking to a little girl who looks very much like you. You have something very important to tell her about picking her eye-lashes because nobody understands that problem better than you do. So you just sit there quietly and tell her all about it."*

On occasion, an adult who stutters comes to me for hypnotherapy. I will often send him back in time to talk to the child he was when the stuttering began, the child who had scarcely learned to talk but had so much to say that the words tumbled over each other in his frustration at being unable to get them all said. He can explain to the child that the words will still be there waiting to be heard even if he speaks a little slower. Often this simple exercise will break the stuttering cycle, and hypnosis can promote further relaxation and fluent speech.

For children who bite their nails or pick their eyelashes or pull their hair out, I invented a Magic Barrier. In hypnosis, we paint a magic invisible fluid over the lashes or nails or hair, and when it dries—and this happens in mere seconds—it provides a barrier that no one can see. But every time the hands of the nailbiter or lash picker or hairpuller stray, even when they are not thinking about it at all, the barrier stops them cold. Just clanging up against that barrier makes the child think about what he is doing. It is a method of establishing a subconscious reminder, an alarm system so that the child can take over his own responsibility for his habit.

Chapter Eleven

The Future

There is so much more to learn about hypnosis and the whole field of psycho-neuro-immunology. Fortunately, there is much on-going research so we can look forward to some significant breakthroughs in the near future. People such as Barry Wyke (M.D., F.R.S.C.) in England have discovered that the hypnotic state has to do with an interruption of the second to last nerve cell connection in the nerve pathway, but we still have to learn what this interruption is. Dabney Ewen's work with burn patients has told us much more about the effect of hypnosis on inflamatory response.

But we need more research on how pain is interfered with, and how the immunological system responds to this interference. We need research into the real nature of the neurotransmitters, we need to identify the pathways that they take in the body, and we need to understand how we can influence them.

Enough studies have been done to indicate that there is a positive correlation between the progress of cancer and the use of hypnosis, particularly with children. Now we need to know more about how we can change our basic biochemistry or our immunological response so that malignant cells can be taken care of and the cancer regresses. Many people in medicine—some operating intiutively and others operating on knowledge gained through research—believe that cancers form not because something bad happens, but because *some good thing stops happening*. But what we need to know is why those good things stop happening. *What can the individual do within himself to get those good things happening again, or to prevent them from stopping in the first place? How can we interfere positively with that cycle?*

We know that cancers frequently happen after the individual has suffered some other serious illness or emotional loss. Does this happen because the onslaught has become too overwhelming for the body to cope with? For example, perhaps you have picked up a virus infection that has interfered with your cell metabolism in some way, or perhaps you are extremely fatigued as the result of emotional stress, or maybe you have an endocrine imbalance and need thyroid replacement. Do these things use up the body's resources so that one of the little cancers that the body makes all the time gets a chance to take hold? If this is so, *what can we do to reverse the process?*

Many lay people are wiser than their physicians because they allow themselves to pay attention to their intuition or inner voices, so they don't have to bother trying to answer all these questions in scientific terms. They just *KNOW*, and they respond to their bodies' needs intuitively. But research is a very comforting thing, especially for doctors. They can feel more comfortable in using techniques like hypnotherapy once they are sure there is a real, scientifically proven reason for it. Consequently, as researchers get the answers to these questions, doctors will have more information to make use of in the operating room, in childbirth, in managing auto-immune diseases, and coping with stress. And more information to give you, their patients.

But all the information in the world is wasted if it is not used. The responsibility is yours.

*   *   *

About The Author

Doctor Marlene Elva Hunter was born in 1931. At nine years of age she decided to become a doctor, but was delayed in carrying out her plan until after the birth of her sons (Miles in 1955, and Leslie in 1959). At the beginning of her second year of medical school, her lawyer-husband John Hunter died suddenly from a brain hemorrhage.

In 1967, on completion of her internship at St. Paul's Hospital in Vancouver, she and her children left for India where she was to serve in a mission hospital. However, because of visa problems, she was seconded to Kenya instead where she served for three and a half years at the Presbyterian Church of East Africa Hospital at Tumutumu in the heart of the Mau Mau-Kikuyu territory.

On her return to Canada, she set up practice in West Vancouver and joined the staff of the Lions Gate Hospital. In 1972, she married widower Redner Jones and with this marriage acquired three daughters.

Marlene Elva Hunter

Bachelor of Arts, Doctor of Medicine, Certificant of the College of Family Physicians of Canada

Chief of General Practice at Lions Gate Hospital from 1975 to 1979 (Deputy Chief of Medicine from 1974 to 1975)

Clinical Assistant Professor in the Department of Family Practice, University of B.C. Faculty of Medicine, lecturing on stress and on hypnosis in the Behavioural Medicine seminars. (Also accepts family practice residents on the Praeceptorship Program.)

Well-known and respected in the medical community for her work in counselling and hypnotherapy, she has done extensive referral work for the past ten years.

Member of the American Society of Clinical Hypnosis, the International Society of Hypnosis, and the Swedish Society of Clinical and Experimental Hypnosis.

President of the Canadian Society of Clinical Hypnosis, B.C. Division, (previously on executive for five years), and has been on the teaching faculty for six years.

She serves on the Joint Conference Advisory Committee for the College of Family Physicians of B.C., on the Executive of the Board of the B.C. Chapter of the College of Family Physicians as Secretary-Treasurer and on the Medical Advisory Committee of the Canadian Cancer Society (B.C. Division) as the respresentative of the Board of the College of Family Physicians.

She was the Scientific Program Chairman for the provincial annual meeting of the College of Family Physicians (B.C. Chapter) and Section of General Practice of the B.C. Medical Association, (1981) and chairman of the Hypnosis Section of the Canada West Medical Congress held in Vancouver May 31 -June 4, 1982. She also holds this position for the next Canada West Medical Congress, to be held in 1986.

She was Scientific Program Chairman for B.C. for the joint meeting of the Hawaiian Academy of General Practice and the College of Family Practioners (B.C. Division)/Section of General Practice, B.C. Medical Association, in Hawaii, February, 1983.

She was on the local arrangements committee for the National Meeting of the College of Family Physicians of Canada in Vancouver in May, 1980 and chairman of the Local Arrangements Committee for the national meeting in July, 1984.

She was organizer and chairman of the annual refresher course in Family Practice at Lions Gate Hospital from 1975 to 1979.

She has served on numerous hospital committees including Child abuse, Palliative care, Abortion, Continuing Medical Education and Public Health.

Papers:

At the 1st European Congress of Hypnosis in Psychotherapy and Psychosomatic Medicine, Malmo, Sweden (1978) "Hypnosis in General Practice" and "Descriptive Body Terminology as an Indication of Dysfunction".

At the Annual Scientific Session of the College of Family
Physicians of Canada, Ottawa, Ontario, (1979),
"Hypnotherapy as an aid in Sexual Dysfunction".

At the 2nd European Congress of Hypnosis in Psychotherapy
and Psychosomatic Medicine, Dubrovnik,
Yugoslavia, (1980), "Hypnosis in an Extended
Care Unit".

At the 24th Annual Scientific Session of the American
Society of Clinical Hypnosis, Boston, U.S.A.,
(1981) "Hypnosis as a learning tool in dyslexic
adolescents".

At the 25th Annual Scientific Session of the American Society
of Clinical Hypnosis, Denver, U.S.A. (1982),
"Hypnosis as a learning tool in dyslexic
adolescents: a Follow-up"
"Groups and Hypnosis for Habit Control".

At the 26th Annual Scientific Session of the American Society
of Clinical Hypnosis, Dallas, U.S.A., (1983)
"Teaching Hypnosis in a Family Practice Unit"
(with Dr. Carol Herbert)
"Spiralling, Holograms, and the Paradox of the
Cocoon-Three Metaphors for Hypnosis".

She has been frequently interviewed on television and radio,
and has lectured and led workshops in the community especially for the Women's Resource Centre at Capilano College.

Index